PROFILES OF
LUTHERANS
IN THE U·S·A·

PROFILES OF LUTHERANS IN THE U·S·A·

Who they are,
where they live,
what they believe,
how they participate
in church and community

CARL F. REUSS

AUGSBURG Publishing House • Minneapolis

PROFILES OF LUTHERANS IN THE U.S.A.

Copyright © 1982 Aid Association for Lutherans

Library of Congress Catalog Card No. 82-70947

International Standard Book No. 0-8066-1922-8

Scripture quotations unless otherwise noted are from the Revised Standard Version of the Bible, copyright 1946, 1952, and 1971 by the Division of Christian Education of the National Council of Churches.

Manufactured in the United States of America

Contents

Introduction   **7**

1   An Interpretive Summary   **11**

2   Being Lutheran   **19**

3   Religious Experiences and Worship Practices   **35**

4   Members of a Congregation   **45**

5   Involvement in the Community   **57**

6   Household Income and Giving Patterns   **73**

7   Residence and Mobility   **81**

8   Who Are the Lutherans?   **91**

Appendix A
Methods Used in the Study   **103**

Appendix B
Profiles of Lutherans Questionnaire   **107**

Appendix C
Profiles of Lutherans Data   **121**

Introduction

In the pages which follow are sketched some *profiles* of Lutherans in the U.S.A. The profiles are neither silhouettes nor portraits. A *silhouette* offers only a bare outline of the subject. A *portrait* provides details needed for a full picture of the subject. A *profile* picks out main features which characterize the form, the shape, and the patterns by which these major features are arranged.

Profiles of Lutherans in the U.S.A. picks out main features which characterize Lutherans living in the United States in 1980. It suggests the forms, the shapes, and the patterns of arrangements among these major features which characterize that body of American people known as Lutherans.

The Lutherans here profiled are the confirmed members of Lutheran congregations, ranging upwards in age from around 13. They are a cross-section of the members of eight Lutheran church bodies, and thus represent 99 percent of U.S. Lutherans. The information about them they themselves provided. (See Appendix A for a description of the methods used in the study.)

Profiles of Lutherans in the U.S.A. thus moves far toward

fulfilling the purposes for which it was designed. The intent was to develop information useful to Lutheran church bodies in:

1. answering basic who, what, where, when, why, and how questions about Lutheran church members, their attitudes, activities, expectations, families, and involvement in church and community.

2. developing church body plans for more effective mission and ministry in the nation, the 50 states, and the thousands of communities where Lutheran congregations are, or might be, located.

Moving to fulfill these purposes, this project developed a major body of data about Lutherans in the United States. There is nothing else quite like it in the Lutheran record books.

Other research projects of course have developed data on Lutherans and Lutheran churches. Most have studied one or another dimension in sharper focus and in greater depth and detail. Some may have contacted more persons, but not from so broad a Lutheran base. Many single out Lutheran data from a larger population, permitting comparisons of Lutherans with neighbors of other religions and of none. A few are rigorously scientific in every detail. Each project adds its gleanings to the harvest of data on Lutherans.

At least five factors mark this *Profiles* project as unique. Together they enhance its usefulness in Lutheran administrative and leadership circles.

1. Officially appointed representatives from each of eight Lutheran church bodies participated in each step of the process, from original exploration of the idea to review of this manuscript prior to its publication.

2. Agreement was reached through discussion and consensus of these representatives on: (a) definition of the purposes of the study, (b) clarification of issues it should address, (c) identification of questions on which data were desired, and (d) adoption of methods for gathering, analyzing, and making use of the data developed through the project.

3. Not only the funding but also, and even more significant, the staff services provided by Aid Association for Lutherans in the person of Dr. Alan C. Klaas gave impetus, leadership, continuity, and supervision to the project on behalf of the steering committee.

4. Comparability with other studies was built into the research design. A number of questions asked are identical with ones asked in other research projects. This dimension of the study awaits further exploration through channels yet being developed.

5. Basic coverage of a broad range of questions rather than in-depth treatment of a few was the deliberate preference that set the dimensions for the study. From the outset the insistence was that the project provide data helpful to the Lutheran church bodies in their services to and on behalf of congregations and the members of these congregations.

The fact that the information on which this analysis is based comes from the members themselves gives special significance to the shape and the content of the data. Differences in patterns of responses by men and women, by laity and clergy, by persons of different age groups, and by persons residing in the four major regions of the United States also profile major features worthy of considered attention. Such evident differences in patterns of responses will be highlighted in the pages which follow.

The four major regions include the following groupings of states:

Northeast: Maine, New Hampshire, Vermont, Massachusetts, Rhode Island, Connecticut, New York, New Jersey, Pennsylvania.

North Central: Ohio, Indiana, Illinois, Michigan, Wisconsin, Minnesota, Iowa, Missouri, North Dakota, South Dakota, Nebraska, Kansas.

South: Delaware, Maryland, District of Columbia, Virginia, West Virginia, North Carolina, South Carolina, Georgia, Florida, Kentucky, Tennessee, Alabama, Mississippi, Arkansas, Louisiana, Oklahoma, Texas.

West: Montana, Idaho, Wyoming, Colorado, New Mexico, Arizona, Utah, Nevada, Washington, Oregon, California, Alaska, Hawaii.

1

An Interpretive Summary

This study highlights some dominant features of the Lutheran profile. It sketches a number of patterns and shapes which appear again and again. These recurring features—warts and wrinkles, smiles and strong-boned structures—clearly characterize the profiles of Lutherans in the U.S.A.

These dominant features—both the weaknesses and the strengths—merit careful consideration. They pose program implications for leaders alike of congregations and of church bodies. Corrective steps are called for to overcome those seen as weaknesses. Renewed efforts to accentuate the strengths in the Lutheran community can have only positive results.

The challenge is to discern which features of the Lutheran profile are strengths, which are weaknesses. So having discerned, the next step is to act with wisdom and with courage in facing directly the implications of each of the ten dominant features of the Lutheran profile identified in this research.

Some Dominant Features

1. *Lutherans are family based.* The great majority of Lutherans were reared as Lutheran or became Lutheran following

their marriage. Most live in husband and wife, parent and children households.

Single persons, separated or divorced persons, and even the widowed are comparatively rare among the active, involved, worship-attending members of Lutheran congregations.

Are Lutheran congregations so built around the husbands, wives, and their children pattern that those who have no spouse or no child feel themselves out of place? Does this family-connected pattern help to explain the larger than usual percentage of older men found in the membership? They still have a living spouse.

2. *The youth-age cycle is critical.* Lutheran congregations appear to have fewer children and fewer elderly in their active membership than is true for the population generally. The elderly often are regarded as "post family" and thus do not feel themselves welcomed. But why proportionately fewer children under five years of age?

Notable differences between young adults (21-35) and persons over 55 merit attention, for example as these appear in:

- their devotional and other religious practices;
- their reading, radio listening, and television viewing patterns;
- their organizational affiliations, the interest and satisfaction they find, and their reasons for participating;
- their attitudes toward roles of men and women and toward basic tenets emphasized in Lutheran churches;
- their financial commitments made to their congregation, to other church-related work, and to agencies in the community at large.

A two-sided critical question for the churches is this: Will the young change their patterns as they age? Or, is the present older generation, reared in another tradition, the last of its kind?

3. *Lutherans are an in-group.* They seek for themselves, their families, and their church. This dominant pattern shows in the use of their time, the organizations they join, the issues which interest them, and the causes to which they contribute.

Even the major functions they expect their congregation to fill relate to self and family—worship, communion, education of their children, programs for their youth, ministries to their members in crises, and ministries to those of their number with special needs.

4. *Lutherans are minimally involved in their communities.* Few are intensely interested in community issues, and only a handful take active roles in dealing with these issues. What issues do interest them are those which affect their families, their children, and their church. They show little interest in the affairs of other institutions beyond church, family, schools, and hospitals.

Neither the time they invest, nor the dollars they contribute, nor their levels of membership activity in either community serving or work-related organizations manifest any high level of involvement in the larger community by Lutherans active and involved in their congregations.

5. *Mobility makes inroads.* Movements of Lutherans over the past ten years have served to intensify the Lutheran membership concentration both in the North Central states and in places of less than 50,000 population, including the open country.

Young adults almost universally move when they complete their educations, begin their careers, and perhaps marry. The large number making multiple moves poses problems both for them and for the institutions of the community, including churches. Those aged 21-27 take the longest time of any age group in registering to vote.

Mobility is interdenominational, too. According to this study Lutherans rarely have been members of another denomination—unless they married a Lutheran. What this study cannot show is how many Lutherans, after marriage, joined their spouse's church—or dropped out of church affiliation. Nor can this study show how many Lutherans, after moving to the Sunbelt, for example, became members of congregations of other denominations. The inroads mobility makes are significant—but barely hinted at in this study.

6. *Lutherans are loyal to their church.* It would be quite upsetting to most Lutherans to be faced with moving to a new community where there is no Lutheran congregation of any church body. Their allegiance is to the Lutheran church rather than to a branch of the Lutheran church. For the majority of Lutheran laity, differences between the Lutheran church bodies are insignificant. This opinion, of course, is not common among Lutheran clergy.

Their church-affiliated groups are the groups to which Lutheran laity give the largest amount of organization time. Their church groups are the ones in which they are especially active. The congregation receives a sizeable gift each week, larger over the year than their contributions to all other causes combined.

7. *Traditional emphases receive muted response.* Lutheran laity today give less than a ringing chorus of assent to traditional doctrinal emphases. Their views on, for example, original sin, salvation through Jesus Christ, good works, the purpose of the gospel, or the ownership of property often are at wide variance from those of the clergy.

Attitudes toward roles of women and men, many of them often theologically undergirded, are shifting to accord more with current cultural emphases.

Earlier emphases on either the "two kingdoms" or the "separation of church and state" are beginning to give way to acceptance of the legitimacy of the church's involvement in social issues that affect families, schools, civil rights, and the church in its institutional relationships with government. There remains, however, a strong skepticism regarding the church's involvement in most other types of social issues.

8. *Devotional practices are limited.* Praying privately and saying grace at meals are part of the daily practice of the majority of Lutherans. The majority also attend worship service each week and receive Holy Communion once a month.

Personal devotions are a daily practice for three in ten, daily reading of the Bible for one in eight, home family devotions for one in twelve. About one in five attends Sunday school or Bible class each week; one in eight listens to a religious radio program and one in fourteen watches a religious television program each week.

The gap between what is preached as desirable and what is practiced in reality is sizeable.

9. *Lutherans are not everywhere alike.* Regional differences at times are great. Loyalty to the church and its institutions seems less, the impact of cultural forces greater, in the Northeast than in the other regions of the United States. Perceptions of the role and purposes of the church and agreement with basic Lutheran doctrinal emphases show some regional differences. Differences between the Northeast and the West usually are the most notable.

10. *Clergy and laity lead different life-styles.* Though their respective households may be members of the same congregation there often are considerable differences between clergy and laity. These differences include, but are not limited to, such matters as:

- frequency of and distance involved in mobility;
- types of organizations of which they are members;
- understanding the roles and purposes of the church;
- the ways in which they use their time and involve themselves in the organizations of which they are members;
- the attitudes they hold toward a number of issues, causes, and concerns;
- personal devotional practices and corporate expressions of their faith;
- financial support of the church, beginning with the congregation but extending outward to the local, the national, and international reaches of the church's total ministry.

Some Program Implications

Challenges abound in each of these ten themes found to recur in the data developed in *Profiles of Lutherans in the*

U.S.A. They force anew the question: "What does it mean to be a Lutheran?" The evidence is strong that Lutherans see their church membership as a matter of *belonging*. The church serves to bond family and neighborhood in a commitment to conserve those values regarded as God-pleasing. The evidence is minimal, however, that Lutherans seek from their church *meaning* for the whole of life, including its total community dimensions.

Is it enough to gather for worship and the sacraments, to provide a Christian education for the children and a peer group organization for the youth, and to minister to the hurting and the handicapped in the membership? Is being a Lutheran a private, in-group, family privilege reserved for one's own branch of the community of faith?

What about scattering into the community? Does concern for persons in crises or persons with special needs limit itself to fellow Lutherans? Or does it extend to any human being hurting or handicapped, near or far, of another religion or of no religion? How does being a Lutheran shape the nature and the quality of one's involvement in the larger community? How does the church involve itself in the issues of community life so as not to leave the impression that these are matters solely for the individual?

These are questions which challenge every branch and structure, every bureau and department, every congregation of the Lutheran church bodies. They pose issues of mission growth and development, of parish and theological education, of evangelical witness and community action, of stewardship and fellowship, of publications and public communication, of higher education and social service, of confessional integrity and ecumenical involvement.

In the final analysis the questions find their answers in the foundations of the faith. Our faith forces us to see ourselves in relationship with God, neighbor, nature, and the institutions of the social order. Our faith confesses the Father's creative and sustaining providence, the Son's redemption from our captivity to sin and death, the Spirit's power for a new life of service through participation in the structures of church and society. Our faith commits us to proclaim in word and deed, not only across the seas but beginning in our own communities, the gospel of forgiveness and life everlasting in and through Jesus Christ our Lord.

Wise planning for Lutheran greater effectiveness in mission and ministry will combine these theological fundamentals with the practical realities that *Profiles* has sketched. Such planning will build on the evident strengths and will work to overcome the evident weaknesses of that body of people known as Lutherans. The greatest human asset they bring is their desire to be faithful to their Lord. Of all other qualities, that which most marks Lutheran congregations and Lutheran people is *faithfulness*. In such soil much can be sown. From such soil much will grow. It is in the congregation that the tilling of this soil first is done.

2

Being Lutheran

How do today's Lutherans come to be Lutheran? Primarily through their families.

How strongly Lutheran do they feel themselves to be? The majority would be quite upset if they had to move to a community that has no Lutheran church. Only a minority regard differences among Lutheran church bodies as significant.

How well informed are they on their church? Well informed, because of parish papers, their church-body publications, and their pastor.

What views do they hold on roles of women and men? That depends on whether they are young or old, women or men, Northeasterners or Westerners, Southerners or Midwesterners.

What positions do they take on some Lutheran doctrinal emphases? Often at quite some variance from those of their pastors!

Specifics follow.

Denominational Experience

Being Lutheran today is virtually a family affair. Three of every four Lutherans have been raised from childhood as Lutherans. Another 15 percent became Lutheran as a result of a marriage relationship. Thus, 90 percent of today's Lutherans are family-undergirded.

This national average is strongly influenced by the Lutheran membership strength in the North Central region. Here, 78 percent of today's Lutherans were reared as Lutherans. In the other three regions about 66 percent of today's Lutherans have been Lutheran from childhood. Marriage, nevertheless, is the second most important factor in a person's becoming Lutheran in each of the four regions. Totaling the "reared" and "marriage" as family-related reasons for being Lutheran today gives this regional picture of family influence:

Northeast—78%   South—85%
North Central—93%   West—82%

The influence of friends and acquaintances is a distant third factor in a person's being Lutheran today. This factor ranges between two percent in the North Central and ten percent in the Northeast. In the South and West it stands at five percent. The direct influence of the pastor or of the program of the congregation is a minimal two to four percent. The individual initiative of the person seeking out a church and choosing a Lutheran congregation is, relatively speaking, twice as important as pastor or program. This is not to deny, however, that the pastor and the program may have been important. It suggests that the Lutheran practices and emphases were the more attractive to the person seeking out a church.

Present-day Lutherans not Lutheran from childhood likely were Methodist (7%) or Baptist, Presbyterian, or Roman Catholic (3% each). Former Baptists are especially numerous among Lutherans in the South (11%). Only seven percent of today's Lutherans cite no denominational background within which they were reared. This is more true in the West, where 13 percent cite no denominational background.

Religiously mixed marriages make up just over half of the

marriages of Lutherans in every region of the U.S.A. except the North Central. Even here, over 40% of the marriages cross denominational lines. Lutheran women are more likely than Lutheran men to marry a non-Lutheran spouse (53% and 39% respectively). Young adults (21-35) in the majority of cases (52%) marry a non-Lutheran. Lutherans over 35 years of age, however, in at least 55 percent of the cases married a fellow Lutheran.

Roman Catholics (10% of the wives, 12% of the husbands) are the largest church group with whom Lutherans marry, closely followed by Methodists (8% of the wives, 11% of the husbands). Marriages with Roman Catholics are especially numerous in the Northeast (17% of the spouses) and among young adults aged 21-35 (18% of the spouses). In the West, for 20 percent of the spouses no denominational heritage is given.

Lutheran clergy, as might be expected, overwhelmingly (92%) were reared as Lutherans and in 80 percent of the cases married a Lutheran spouse. Half of the non-Lutheran spouses were either Methodist or Presbyterian.

Lutheran Commitment

Lutherans have a high degree of commitment to the Lutheran church. Their commitment is more to the Lutheran church as a whole than to their individual Lutheran church body.

Support for this observation comes from answers to two related questions. One asked how upsetting it would be to the respondents if they had to move to another area which had no congregation of their own Lutheran church body but did have a Lutheran congregation. The other asked how upsetting it would be if there were no Lutheran congregation of any kind. The majority of Lutherans (54%) find the first possibility not upsetting, but the second very upsetting (57%).

Women find either prospect more upsetting than do men, as the following tabulation shows:

	Women	Men
Lutheran Church But Not Own Body		
Not upsetting	51%	58%
Very upsetting	26%	20%
No Lutheran Church of Any Kind		
Not upsetting	22%	27%
Very upsetting	62%	51%

Of the several age groups, the youth (under 21) find the prospect of moving to a community without a Lutheran church the most upsetting. Some 68 percent express this sentiment. Regionally, Northeastern Lutherans are less upset than are Lutherans in the North Central and South at the prospect of moving to a new community which has no Lutheran congregation either of their own church body or of any other.

Perceived Differences Among Lutheran Church Bodies

Asked how different the "Lutheran church bodies are from each other," the plurality (39%) of Lutheran laity answers "I do not know." Nearly one in four (23%) feels the differences at most to be but *slight*. Another nearly one-fourth (22%) feels that Lutheran church bodies are *moderately different*. Only one in six (16%) Lutheran lay persons regards the several Lutheran church bodies as *quite* or *extremely different* from one another.

Perhaps one may group together and regard as significant those differences labeled *moderate, quite,* or *extreme*. By this criterion only two Lutheran lay persons in every five (38%) regard Lutheran church body differences as significant. Lutheran clergy feel otherwise. Nearly four of every five (76%) regard Lutheran church body differences as significant.

In terms of special groups the majority of youth and of Northeastern Lutherans "do not know" how different the Lutheran church bodies are from each other. A plurality of members of the other age groups and of the other regions shares this nonopinion.

In the other direction, however, 45 percent of persons aged 36-55, and an identical percent of Lutherans in the West, feel that Lutheran church body differences indeed are significant.

Asked whether the perceived differences between the Lutheran church bodies are doctrinal, political/organizational, or historical/ancestral, clergy and laity answer differently. Among those Lutherans who believe that the differences are only slight, the laity regard the doctrinal and historical as closely equal factors. For them the political factor is in close third place. Clergy who believe the differences to be slight regard the historical/ancestral as the major factor, and put doctrinal matters in distant third place.

Others believe that Lutheran church body differences are moderate. Among them, laity regard doctrinal matters as the important, but not majority factor. They regard the political and historical factors as not far behind in importance. Among those believing the differences to be moderate, clergy again rate the historical as the largest single factor but increase the rating they give to third-place doctrinal matters.

There is no doubt among either laity or clergy who regard Lutheran church bodies as quite or extremely different from one another that the critical factor is doctrinal matters. Neither the political nor the historical factor rates high in their minds.

A more complex picture of this set of Lutheran church body differences as perceived by clergy and laity appears in Table 1. It shows the percentage weighting each group gives to the three factors contributing to the church body differences.

Notice that as the perceived degree of difference intensifies, the weight given the doctrinal factor shifts from under 30% to over 59%. This is true for both laity and clergy. Notice, too, the relatively high weight given the historical factor by those who regard Lutheran church bodies' differences as slight. This is especially felt among the clergy. Notice, further, the high percentage of "no answer" given to the political factor by those who feel Lutheran church bodies are extremely different. It

**Table 1. Degrees of Difference Perceived Between Lutheran
Church Bodies, and Percentage Weights Assigned
Three Major Factors by Laity and Clergy**

Degree of Difference Perceived and Percentage Weight Given to Factor	Factors in Differences Perceived					
	Doctrinal		Political		Historical	
	Laity %	Clergy %	Laity %	Clergy %	Laity %	Clergy %
Slightly different						
No answer	20	11	33	9	25	5
Under 30%	36	76	31	36	27	15
30-59%	25	6	23	44	29	44
Over 59%	19	7	13	11	19	36
Moderately different						
No answer	11	5	20	4	17	4
Under 30%	29	54	39	40	39	32
30-59%	34	32	29	43	33	43
Over 59%	26	9	12	13	11	21
Quite different						
No answer	9	2	28	12	24	9
Under 30%	18	26	42	57	48	55
30-59%	27	30	25	20	24	28
Over 59%	46	42	5	11	4	8
Extremely different						
No answer	17	0	40	34	38	26
Under 30%	11	13	37	52	47	55
30-59%	22	12	16	10	12	15
Over 59%	50	75	7	4	3	4

suggests that for many who feel thus, the political/organizational factor is of minimal significance.

Limitations of the available data prevent making any meaningful comparisons between and among the major age groups in terms of their perceived degrees of difference among Lutheran churches.

Information About Church Body

Virtually all Lutherans (88%) feel that they are informed on the activities of their church body. Their primary sources of information are the congregation's bulletin or newsletter, their church body publication, and the pastor. Age and regional variations are minimal.

Clergy universally (99%) feel they are informed on the activities of their church body, relying primarily on their church body publication for their needed information.

Periodicals Read

Six of the periodicals listed on the questionnaire are widely recognized by Lutheran laity: the *Lutheran,* the *Lutheran Standard, Scope, Portals of Prayer, Guideposts,* and the *Lutheran Witness.* Each is known to at least 19 percent. Two other publications—*Decision* magazine and district newsletters —are known to at least 11% of all Lutheran laity.

Regional variations of course occur. The *Lutheran* is dominant in the Northeast and is the strongest of the three church body periodicals in the south. The *Lutheran Standard* is strongest in the North Central and the West. The *Lutheran Witness,* in turn, is second to the *Lutheran* in the South and to the *Lutheran Standard* in the North Central and West. What this pattern reflects, of course, is the tendency for church members to know and read their own church body publications.

Awareness of *Portals of Prayer* regionally is akin to the *Witness,* of *Scope* to the *Standard. Guideposts* enjoys a nationwide awareness, regional differences among Lutherans being minimal. *Decision* also shows few regional differences in Lutheran awareness of the magazine. District newsletters are least known in the Northeast.

Awareness of the publication is one matter. Even more significant is the level of readership of the publication. Details are provided in Table 2, showing readership levels for men and women, four age groups, and the clergy.

Table 2. Levels of Readership of Periodicals Widely Circulated Among Lutherans, by Gender, Age, and Clergy

Periodical and Level of Readership			Percent of Those Mentioning Periodical				
	Male	*Female*	*Under 21*	*21-35*	*36-55*	*Over 55*	*Clergy*
Lutheran							
Seldom open	10	8	31	11	6	4	2
Skim titles, headlines	14	10	19	19	16	3	1
One or two articles	42	39	30	51	42	38	30
Whole issue	34	43	20	19	36	55	67
Lutheran Standard							
Seldom open	12	12	32	25	9	3	2
Skim titles, headlines	13	5	10	14	12	4	3
One or two articles	43	47	52	45	51	41	30
Whole issue	32	36	6	16	28	52	65
Lutheran Witness							
Seldom open	13	12	35	24	8	4	1
Skim titles, headlines	18	16	26	28	15	10	11
One or two articles	43	43	32	33	56	35	40
Whole issue	26	29	7	15	21	51	48
Scope							
Seldom open	30	18	44	39	22	8	22
Skim titles, headlines	14	6	21	12	11	6	12
One or two articles	25	24	22	25	24	25	44
Whole issue	31	52	13	24	43	61	22
Portals of Prayer							
Seldom open	18	14	51	29	12	3	16
Skim titles, headlines	9	5	12	11	6	3	2
One or two articles	36	30	17	34	43	21	27
Whole issue	37	51	20	26	39	73	55
Guideposts							
Seldom open	22	15	28	35	15	7	26
Skim titles, headlines	13	8	15	17	8	7	14
One or two articles	35	17	31	15	23	28	39
Whole issue	30	60	26	33	54	58	21
Decision							
Seldom open	38	33	65	65	31	12	41
Skim titles, headlines	18	14	26	8	22	12	25
One or two articles	31	34	9	19	34	48	20
Whole issue	13	19	0	8	13	28	14

Table 2 — *Continued*

Percent of Those Mentioning Periodical

Periodical and Level of Readership	Male	Female	Under 21	21-35	36-55	Over 55	Clergy
District Newsletters							
Seldom open	9	10	41	15	4	1	0
Skim titles, headlines	15	16	20	21	23	3	7
One or two articles	38	26	24	32	34	25	18
Whole issue	38	48	15	32	39	71	75

Several general patterns are clear:

1. Without exception women more often than men read the whole issue of each of the publications.

2. Older people over 55 are the most likely, and youth under 21 the least likely, to read the whole issue. (The *Lutheran* is the sole exception; its youth readership level is slightly larger than its young adult readership level.)

3. Clergy are more likely than male laity to read the whole issue. The sole exceptions are *Scope* and *Guideposts*.

4. Periodicals with significant devotional content, such as *Portals of Prayer, Scope*, and *Guideposts* attract the majority of women to read the whole of each issue.

5. District newsletters and the church body papers, especially the *Lutheran* and the *Lutheran Standard*, enjoy the highest levels of whole issue readership by the clergy.

Members of the clergy frequently cite also a number of other publications. These, with the percent of clergy naming them, include: *Affirm* (26%), *Christian Century* (28%), *Christian Herald* (10%), *Christian News* (28%), *Christianity Today* (33%), *Interchange* (17%), *Missouri in Perspective* (28%), and *Reporter* (26%).

Clergy readership of the whole issue of these periodicals is particularly strong for the *Reporter* (71%). Both *Missouri in Perspective* and *Christian Century* enjoy a 40 percent whole-issue readership level. Four publications—*Affirm, Christian News, Christianity Today,* and *Interchange*—range between 21 and 25 percent of their recipients reading the whole issue. Although *Christian Herald* is mentioned by ten percent of the clergy, 68 percent of them seldom open it, and only five percent read its issues in their entirety.

Roles of Women

Lutherans reveal a variety of attitudes about men's and women's roles, rights, and responsibilities. These issues and answers relate at least tangentially to emphases often included in traditional Lutheran teachings. For that reason, responses to eight questions dealing with current issues of women's roles are considered in connection with being Lutheran.

As would be expected, attitudes of men and women as well as of the young and the old differ on many issues. Regional variations also appear. In some instances there are notable differences between the views of clergy and of laity. In others, clergy and laity are in substantial agreement.

On one issue there is a 90 percent or better agreement across the Lutheran spectrum of men and women, laity and clergy, ages, and regions. Not over four percent disagree with the proposition: Compared with men, women should receive equal pay for equal work.

A second proposition is supported by a 50 to 55 percent majority of men and women, clergy, persons over 35 years of age, and by Lutherans in every region. Only persons under 36 disagree more often than they agree. Persons over 55 give the strongest, a 66 percent, agreement. Except for the young, Lutherans generally agree, therefore, that: Raising children is the most important thing a woman can do.

On three propositions at least a plurality, usually a majority, of Lutherans across the spectrum *disagree.* (Those over 55, as the exception, are almost evenly divided on each issue.) Lutherans, by and large, do not believe that:

113. It is somehow unnatural to place women in positions of authority over men.

114. It is more unfair for a woman to desert her family than for a man to do so.

116. Women rely more on intuition and less on reason than men do.

Gender, regional, and age variations are evident in how Lutherans view these next three propositions:

115. Some equality in the marriage is a good thing, but by and large the husband should have the final say in family matters.

117. A mother should have primary responsibility for the care and nurture of children.

118. A married woman with small children has as much right as her husband to work outside the home.

Men agree, women and the clergy disagree, with the first two propositions (#115, #117). Joining the men with more votes on the *agree* than the *disagree* side of these first two propositions are Lutherans over 55 years of age and those in the North Central region. Lutherans in the West are almost evenly divided on both propositions, and those in the South are evenly divided on the mother's prime responsibility for children (#117). On this same issue persons in the 36-55 age range tilt toward agreement.

Proposition 118 is one with which men disagree, women agree. Joining the women in agreement are persons under 36 years of age and persons in the Northeast, South, and West. Closely divided between agreement and disagreement are the middle-aged (36-55) and the clergy.

Table 3 provides supporting details for gender, selected ages, and clergy.

Table 3. Women's Roles: Attitudes Toward Selected Situations

				Age	Over
Statement of situation	Men	Women	Clergy	21-35	55
113. It is somehow unnatural to place women in positions of authority over men.					
Agree	34	28	27	20	41
Disagree	43	57	59	64	40
114. It is more unfair for a woman to desert her family than for a man to do so.					
Agree	24	32	14	19	38
Disagree	48	47	69	59	38
115. Some equality in the marriage is a good thing, but by and large the husband should have the final say in family matters.					
Agree	41	35	38	32	38
Disagree	35	47	46	53	36
116. Women rely more on intuition and less on reason than men do.					
Agree	37	27	30	18	41
Disagree	37	57	47	61	39
117. A mother should have primary responsibility for the care and nurture of children.					
Agree	48	35	34	32	46
Disagree	33	46	48	52	35
118. A married woman with small children has as much right as her husband to work outside the home.					
Agree	36	48	43	60	33
Disagree	50	38	42	28	51

The heading spans: **Percent of Group Agreeing or Disagreeing**

Basic Lutheran Emphases

A series of seven statements addressed issues of special emphasis in Lutheran doctrinal teachings. Respondents were asked to indicate shades of agreement or disagreement with each. It is clear that there are widespread variations in Lutheran understanding or acceptance of these belief statements.

Two statements elicit an agreement by laity of at least 70 percent:

77. Property (house, automobile, money, investments, etc.) belongs to God; we only hold it in trust for God. (agree, 73%; disagree, 13%)

72. Only those who believe in Jesus Christ as their Savior can go to heaven. (agree, 71%; disagree, 18%)

On the property ownership issue, clergy agree almost universally (97%). On the second (#72), clergy views are close to those of the laity, 75 percent agreeing, 18 percent disagreeing.

Three statements with which the majority of laity agree are:

73. A child is already sinful at birth (agree, 63%; disagree, 27%)

75. Although there are many religions in the world, most of them lead to the same God (agree, 58%; disagree, 32%)

74. The main emphasis of the Gospel is on God's rules for right living (agree, 55%; disagree, 34%)

Clergy viewpoints are more pronounced—and different. Some 96 percent agree with the first statement (#73), some 96 percent disagree with the third (#74), and 85 percent disagree with the second statement (#75). Clergy views, one may assume, represent the current basic Lutheran teaching. The rather remarkable differences between clergy and laity views merit greater, in-depth study as to their causes and probable consequences.

A statement relating to God's acceptance of a person's best efforts is phrased "76. God is satisfied if a person lives the best life one can." Laity are almost equally divided between agreeing (43%) and disagreeing (44%) with this statement. Clergy disagree by a 92 to 7 percent ratio.

Four of these questions—74, 75, 76, and 77—were asked in 1970 and reported in *A Study of Generations* by Strommen, Brekke, Underwager, and Johnson (Augsburg Publishing House, 1972). Over the decade there was minimal shift in the views of Lutherans on the emphases of the gospel (#74). Regarding all religions leading to the same God (#75), agreement shifted downward from 72 to 58 percent, disagreement upward from 23 to 32 percent. There was a similar, though much smaller, downward shift in agreeing that God is satisfied with one's best (#76—50% to 43%). And, there was a shift toward greater agreement that property belongs to God, 69 percent and 73 percent. Those disagreeing with this belief decreased in greater ratio, from 24 percent in 1970 to 13 percent in 1980. At the risk of misusing labels, these shifts over the decade appear to move in a "conservative" direction.

On another statement laity respond with what may be regarded as a more traditional view than that of the clergy. "71. The account of Adam and Eve falling into sinfulness is simply a story which did NOT take place in reality" relates to ways of interpreting the Bible. Laity strongly disagree (69%) with this view, only 19 percent agreeing. Clergy also disagree, but less emphatically; 55 percent disagree, but as many as 40 percent agree.

The views of men and women on these seven statements differ little. Two exceptions occur. Women are somewhat more likely than men to agree that all religions lead to the same God and that God is satisfied if one does one's best.

Variations among age groups in response to these statements are comparatively minimal. Regional variations are much more marked than on most other questions. Table 4 provides details for the under-21 and the over-55 age groups and for each of the regions.

Table 4. Acceptance of Some Lutheran Beliefs

	Percent of Group Indicating Agreement or Disagreement					
Statement of belief	Under 21	Over 55	North-east	North Central	South	West
77. Property belongs to God.						
Agree	55	79	57	78	72	75
Disagree	19	9	24	10	13	13
72. Only believers in Jesus Christ can go to heaven.						
Agree	60	75	58	75	70	73
Disagree	21	16	29	15	20	18
73. Child sinful at birth.						
Agree	61	67	39	70	62	65
Disagree	25	21	50	20	27	24
75. Religions lead to same God.						
Agree	60	55	72	55	59	50
Disagree	27	33	20	34	32	38
74. Gospel is God's rules.						
Agree	41	66	64	54	56	45
Disagree	32	27	24	35	34	46
76. God satisfied with one's best.						
Agree	45	39	61	38	47	36
Disagree	33	47	27	48	39	54
71. Adam and Eve falling into sin not real event.						
Agree	10	19	33	15	20	15
Disagree	78	65	53	73	68	74

Marked age-group variations appear on statements 77, 74, and 76. On the first and third statements older persons seem to be closer to the traditional Lutheran emphasis. On the statement relating to the emphasis of the gospel, youth are closer to the traditional Lutheran emphasis.

Differences between the Northeast and the West are especially great on statements relating to: all religions lead to the same God, the emphasis of the gospel, God being satisfied with one's best, and the historicity of the account of Adam and Eve. In general, Lutherans in the North Central and the West hold more closely to traditional Lutheran emphases than do those in the other two regions, especially the Northeast.

Postscript

Strong ties to their family and long-time loyalty to their Lutheran church mark Lutherans. Mostly they do not see Lutheran church bodies as markedly different from one another.

The ofttimes marked differences between clergy and laity on some of the basic belief statements offer a signal. They suggest an erosion of laity understanding and acceptance of these Lutheran emphases. Implications are clear for confirmation instruction, for instruction of adults from another denomination, seeking to become members of a Lutheran congregation, and for possible refresher courses for all members on the fundamentals of the faith as taught in the Lutheran Confessions. This is crucial if the church is to be not only for belonging but also for giving meaning to the issues and questions of the age.

3

Religious Experiences
and Worship Practices

Religion is very important to Lutherans. Their religion does not often express itself in "born again" or charismatic experiences. Nor are Lutherans devotees of religiously oriented radio and television programs. They are, however, quite comfortable with orders of worship other than the regular liturgy. The majority likely attend Sunday worship, pray privately each day, offer grace at meals, and receive Communion not oftener than once a month. The majority likely do not attend Sunday school, experience family devotions, or read the Bible with any frequency. Attending church, for Lutherans, is a matter of their relationship with God.

Influence of Religion

Their religious beliefs are "very important" to most Lutheran laity. This is more so among women than men, 76 percent to 68 percent. It is more true of the older person than of the younger—80 percent of those over 55 years of age, 55 percent of those under 21 regarding their religious beliefs as "very important." It is somewhat less true of Lutherans in the Northeast (66%) than for Lutherans in the other three regions (73% to 75%).

This "very important" rating is much higher than that given to a comparable question in a 1980 Gallup Poll. (See *Religion in America, 1981,* Princeton Religion Research Center, Inc., pp. 39-41.) In that poll, 57 percent of the Lutherans rated their religion as "very important" in their lives. For all Americans, 62 percent of the women, 48 percent of the men, so rated the importance of religion in their lives. For the nation as a whole, religion was notably "very important" to those over 50 more than to those under 30 (65% and 43% respectively). The "very important" ratio was lowest in the East (49%) though only slightly lower than in the West (51%).

It is interesting to note that though the *Profiles* ratings of "very important" are much higher than those of the Gallup Poll, the patterns of differences between the sexes, the ages, and the regions are similar. Perhaps a portion of the difference in relative scores stems from the variation in the question. *Profiles* asked the importance of "religious beliefs," Gallup of "religion." The latter may connote one's religious organization, church, or synagogue—the corporate rather than the personal.

As to whether religion is increasing or losing in influence on American life, Lutherans divide fairly evenly. Just under 40 percent think it is increasing, just over 40 percent think that religion is losing, in influence on American life.

Men regard religion as losing rather than increasing in influence by a 45 to 35 percent margin. Women divide evenly, 38 percent to 38 percent. The 21-35 years age group slightly more often regards religion as increasing rather than losing influence, by a 43 to 40 percent margin.

This is the only age group in which this balance in favor of religion's influence occurs. Among the regions, only Lutherans in the West more often see religion as increasing than as losing its influence.

A comparable Gallup Poll question (*Religion in America, 1981,* p. 49) offers a similar pattern, though weighted more heavily to the "losing" influence side. In this poll, men weight their answers 48 to 30 percent on religion's losing rather than increasing in influence. Women divide 45 to 40.

"Born Again" Experience

One-third (35%) of the respondent Lutheran laity have been "born again" or had a "born again" experience. Among the clergy nearly one-half (47%) report such an experience.

Southern and Western Lutherans are more likely than their Northeastern brothers and sisters to feel themselves "born again"—40 percent compared with 30 percent.

Somewhat fewer of the laity, but considerably more of the clergy, have had a religious experience that changed the direction of their lives. Here the ratios are 30 percent for the laity, 56 percent for the clergy. One may surmise that it was such a deeply felt experience that moved the latter to become pastors.

This "born again" or deeply felt religious experience does not, however, cause Lutherans to regard themselves as pentecostal or charismatic. Only one in eleven of the laity, one in fourteen of the clergy, so regard themselves.

Television and Radio Programs

One supposition holds that religiously oriented programs on television and radio attract a considerable audience of church members. The data from this study scarcely support that view. Of the seven programs listed for response, the picture among Lutheran laity of no mention of the program, of tuning in at least several times a year, and of tuning in almost every week is shown in the chart on the next page.

Lutheran clergy appear to prefer Lutheran-sponsored radio or television programs when they tune in to religious broadcasts. They listen to *The Lutheran Hour* and watch *This Is the Life* in ratios quite comparable to those of the laity. For the others they tune in about one-third to one-half as often as do the laity.

Program	% Making No Mention	% At Least Several Times a Year	% Almost Every Week
Billy Graham	39	31	1
The Lutheran Hour	58	23	4
This Is the Life	73	13	2
Robert Schuller	77	11	2
Oral Roberts	66	11	1
Rex Humbard	79	7	1
PTL	84	7	1

Persons over 55 years of age are two to four times as likely as those under 21 to be members of the audience for religious programs on radio or television. Illustrative are the 47 percent of the over 55 age group compared with the 15 percent of those under 21 who tune in to Billy Graham programs at least several times a year. Another illustration: *The Lutheran Hour* attracts 35 percent of the over-55s, nine percent of the under-21s, at least several times a year. The Rex Humbard program is a major exception. There are no age group differences in the Lutheran audience for this program.

A scattering of other programs draws a minimal Lutheran audience. Among them are the Jerry Falwell and the *700 Club* programs. About one in 100 Lutherans named these as programs they watch at least several times a year.

Orders of Worship

Lutheran congregations regularly follow one or two orders of worship when they gather as a community at worship. The majority of Lutherans, nevertheless, during the past year have experienced orders of worship other than the regular liturgy. Their reactions vary.

By and large the Lutheran laity find these out-of-the-ordinary services both satisfying and worshipful. This is much more true for the clergy. Around 70 percent of the clergy, around

40 percent of the laity, consider these nontraditional services both satisfying and worshipful.

As might be expected, persons under the age of 36 are more favorably inclined toward these services than are those over the age of 55. Men are slightly more likely than are women to register their negative feelings.

These impressions are based on some experience with the nontraditional services. One-third of the laity, two-thirds of the clergy, have had at least four experiences with orders of service other than the regular. Youth under 21 years of age are twice as likely as older persons beyond 55 to have had frequently repeated experiences with orders of worship other than the regular.

Specific laity–clergy and age-group data appear in Table 5.

Table 5. Experience During Year with Order of Worship Different from Regular

	Percent of Group Responding Age					
	Laity	Clergy	Under 21	21-35	36-55	Over 55
Number of times experienced						
None and no answer	30	9	17	24	27	39
1-3	38	22	37	41	37	34
4 or more	32	69	46	35	36	27
Find experience satisfying						
Very satisfying	41	73	44	49	43	33
Not satisfying	19	6	12	15	21	21
Find experience worshipful						
Very worshipful	38	71	49	44	39	31
Not worshipful	13	4	10	10	15	13

Note: Intermediate and no-answer percentages not shown for *satisfying* and *worshipful.* Together, they equal the difference between 100 and the sum of "very" plus "not." They represent a significant noncommittal response by the laity, especially those over 55.

Worship Experiences

Lutherans are encouraged to express their faith in a variety of personal and corporate ways. These include attendance at worship and Sunday school, receiving Communion, engaging in personal and family devotions, praying privately, saying grace at mealtime, and reading the Bible.

Whether, and how often, Lutherans practice these expressions of their faith is a significant feature of the Lutheran profile. Table 6 presents pertinent details.

In summary, the majority of Lutheran laity say they attend worship weekly (54%), pray privately each day (61%), daily offer grace at meals (57%), and receive Communion not oftener than once a month (53%). On the other hand, the majority do not attend Sunday school or Bible class (57%) and do not experience family devotions (77%). Not over once a month do the majority read the Bible or practice personal devotions.

Several gender and regional differences not shown in Table 6 merit mention. Women are more likely than men to pray privately each day (67% and 54%) and to engage in personal devotions daily (33% and 24%). Regionally, Lutherans in the South and the West attend Bible class in higher proportions than do their brothers and sisters in the Northeast and North Central regions. Lutherans in the Northeast are less likely than those in the other regions to say grace at meals, to attend worship oftener than once a month, and to attend other religious gatherings as often as six times a year.

The basis for making age-group comparisons shows in Table 6. Weekly worship attendance, for example, is proportionately lowest among young adults (21-35) and highest among the middle-aged (36-55). At least weekly Bible reading is characteristic of 35 percent of those persons over 55 years of age but of only 16 percent of young adults (21-35). Similarly, the elderly are much more likely than are the young adults to pray privately and to practice daily devotions.

As would be expected, clergy far outstrip the laity in wheth-

Table 6. Frequency of Specific Religious Experiences for Laity and for Major Age Groups

Number of Times in Past Year Person Experienced This Religious Practice in Own Life	Percent of Each Group Naming Experience and Frequency				
	Total Laity	Under 21	21-35	36-55	Over 55
Attend worship					
None and no answer	13	12	8	9	18
1-12 times	11	14	18	9	9
13-36 times	22	23	29	22	16
Weekly	54	51	45	60	57
Receive Communion					
None and no answer	9	10	10	6	8
1-12 times	53	55	56	49	55
13-36 times	33	29	31	39	32
Weekly	5	6	3	6	5
Attend Sunday school or Bible class					
None and no answer	57	38	56	54	66
1-12 times	14	31	17	13	12
13-36 times	11	9	11	12	9
Weekly	18	22	16	21	13
Attend religious gathering					
None and no answer	41	28	40	37	47
1-5 times	28	42	31	30	22
6 times or more	31	30	29	33	31
Bible reading					
None and no answer	35	26	32	32	37
1-12 times	27	38	40	27	19
13-36 times	11	16	12	12	9
Weekly or oftener	27	20	16	29	35
Pray privately					
None and no answer	10	5	6	8	12
1-12 times	9	17	10	9	5
13-52 times	20	25	32	22	10
Daily	61	53	52	61	73

Table 6 — *Continued*

Number of Times in Past Year Person Experienced This Religious Practice in Own Life	Total Laity	Under 21	21-35	36-55	Over 55
			Percent of Each Group Naming Experience and Frequency Age Group		
Personal devotions					
None and no answer	38	37	31	35	42
1-12 times	17	30	26	17	8
13-52 times	16	11	24	19	10
Daily	29	22	19	29	40
Grace at meals					
None and no answer	15	8	10	13	18
1-12 times	14	25	18	15	8
13-52 times	14	15	20	11	11
Daily	57	52	52	61	63
Home family devotions					
None and no answer	77	79	74	76	79
1-12 times	9	12	14	11	3
13-52 times	6	5	7	8	5
Daily	8	4	5	5	13
Listen to religious radio					
None and no answer	43	52	54	38	38
1-12 times	36	40	33	41	33
13-36 times	8	4	6	7	10
Weekly or oftener	13	4	7	14	19
Watch religious television					
None and no answer	42	48	46	36	39
1-12 times	45	49	46	50	45
13-36 times	6	1	5	8	6
Weekly or oftener	7	2	3	6	10

er, and how frequently, they engage in the various religious and devotional practices. There is no difference between clergy and laity, however, in their frequency of listening regularly to radio or watching television for the religious programs they offer. Clergy are significantly more aware of the availability of these programs than are laity, more often recognizing the names or personalities of these religious programs.

These data on Lutheran laity in their devotional practices

must give concern to church body leaders. The gap between what is proclaimed as a standard and what is practiced in personal lives is considerable. What must give even greater concern is that these Lutherans probably are more active, more committed, better educated, than are the rank-and-file members of Lutheran congregations.

Reasons for Attending Church

Asked to name the one strongest reason why they attend church, one Lutheran in three is likely to answer "to worship God." One in five will say it's because of the "need to hear God's Word." One in eight will say that they enjoy participating in the services.

When analyzed in broad terms, the strongest reasons why people attend church fall into two categories. One centers around relationship with God. The second centers around self and others. Grouped thus, the following picture emerges for Lutherans in their reasons for attending church.

Related to God
- to worship God—33%
- need to hear God's Word—20%
- to experience the feeling of praising God—10%
- to feel God's presence—9%

Related to Self and Others
- I enjoy participating in the service/hearing the pastor. —13%
- I feel a general sense of obligation to attend.—8%
- Someone requires that I attend.—2%
- I enjoy being with the people (sense of community).—2%

Put in this framework, nearly three of every four Lutherans (72%) attend church for reasons perceived to be God-related. Interestingly, however, 44 percent of those under 21 see their strongest reasons as being related to self and others. In contrast, only 22 percent of those over 35 place their strongest reason on this horizontal axis of self and others.

Postscript

Age and gender considerations clearly are an important sub-feature of the profile of Lutheran religious experiences and worship practices. How age and gender relate to the role of the family in nurturing Christian values and devotional practices is not clear. There are strong hints, however, that Lutheran families regard devotional practices as the individual expression of the family member rather than as a shared family experience. It seems that serious efforts are needed to help the Lutheran family grow in giving its members a shared religious meaning and an outward expression of their faith in Jesus Christ.

4

Members of a Congregation

For Lutherans, being members of a congregation is important. Congregations are felt to exist principally for worship and the sacraments, for Christian education, and for care of members in need. Outreaches in social ministry and involvement in community issues are divisive matters. When crises strike, Lutherans turn in various directions for help, depending on the nature of the need or the type of crisis. The church is but one resource. Patterns of support for the church include pledges and provisions in one's will—but with considerable regional, age, and lay–clergy differences.

Purposes of the Congregation

Asked to name the most important purpose of a congregation, Lutherans resoundingly answer "Sunday morning worship." Some 70 percent name worship as of first importance; another 20 percent place worship in a position of second or third importance.

The other top priority purposes Lutheran laity expect from their congregations, in addition to Sunday morning worship, are Holy Communion and Christian education of children. Each is placed in the top three by a 60 to 90 percent majority.

In the second rank of importance, but belonging in the top six functions, Lutheran laity place three others: members' support for one another in time of need, youth programs, and ministry of service to persons with special needs. Each receives a majority or close to majority support as belonging in the top six and ranking in the fourth to sixth place of importance. The only other function seen as of some importance is Bible study for adults. It receives 42 percent support as belonging in the top six functions, 30 percent placing it in the fourth to sixth rank.

Interesting to note are those functions which at least 80 percent of the laity did *not* place within the top six. For the great majority of laity these activities receive little support:

- fellowship occasions (i.e., dinners, picnics)
- service projects to meet local social concerns
- church-sponsored recreational activities
- weekday prayer or worship services
- small groups for sharing personal insights or concerns
- opportunities to participate in the broader work of the church
- evangelism

It appears clear that laity look to their congregation especially for Sunday morning worship, including Communion, for the education of their children and programs for their youth, and for care and service to their members with special needs. It is an in-group set of personal and family expectations. Neither fellowship nor recreation nor community service nor outreach bulks large in the minds of the laity.

Clergy see the scene somewhat differently. They place Bible study for adults among the top six functions. This would replace youth programs. For sixth place clergy divide their support among: bring new members into the church, opportunities to participate in the broader work of the church, and ministry of service to persons with special needs. Clergy more than laity show a concern for the congregation's purposes of enlarging the vision of Christian faith and life. (See Table 7 for comprehensive data.)

Table 7. Top Six Functions of Congregation as Seen by Laity and Clergy

Function	Percent Placing Function in Top Three		Percent Placing Function in 4-6 Place		Percent Not Listing Function	
	Laity	Clergy	Laity	Clergy	Laity	Clergy
Sunday morning worship	92	92	3	4	5	4
Holy Communion	78	72	11	15	11	13
Christian education of children	61	39	23	43	16	18
Members' support of one another in time of need	12	18	41	45	47	37
Youth programs	7	2	41	17	52	81
Ministry of service to persons with special needs	7	7	41	26	52	67
Bible study for adults	12	28	30	41	58	31
Bring new members into church	7	18	23	24	70	58
Fellowship occasions (dinners, picnics)	3	1	17	12	80	87
Opportunities to participate in broader work of the church	3	6	16	32	81	62
Service projects to meet local social concerns	4	3	11	14	85	83
Weekday prayer or worship services	3	3	8	4	89	93
Small groups for sharing personal insights or concerns	2	3	7	11	91	86
Church-sponsored recreation	1	0	6	1	93	99
Evangelism	1	5	0	1	99	94

A few age variations seem notable. Most interesting is the fact that only among the over-55s does a majority fail to regard the members' support for one another in time of need as belonging in the top six functions of the congregation. The over-55s and the youth (under 21) agree in giving majority support to youth programs as a top-six congregational priority.

Regionally two variations reflect differing emphases. A 50 percent majority in the West support Bible study for adults as a top-six priority for a congregation. Both in the West (58%) and in the Northeast (57%) a strong majority give high priority to members' support for one another in time of need. Further, though the percent is small (21%), more Northeastern Lutherans than those in any other region place service projects to meet local social concerns among the top six functions. In the North Central region 12 percent make this choice.

Involvement in Social Issues

Whether, and if so how, churches should be involved in specific social issues is a matter of some difference of opinion among Lutherans. Differences between laity and clergy are especially great both on specific issues and on manner of involvement. (Refer to Table 8 for specific data.)

At least two of every three lay persons, for example, feel that the church should not be involved in issues of elections and candidates, of business–government relations, or of local zoning laws. At least a majority of laity feel that the church should not be involved in issues of handling of crime and criminals or of medical care.

Clergy feel otherwise. A scant majority (50%) agree on non-involvement in issues of candidates and elections. Strong majorities, ranging from 62 to 80 percent, favor some type of church involvement in each of the other four issues.

Some 60 to 65 percent of the laity believe that some sort of church involvement is appropriate in issues relating to:

- rights of minorities
- substance abuse prevention
- education in schools
- church–government relationships.

Table 8. Acceptable Levels of Church Involvement in Specific Social Issues as Seen by Laity and Clergy

	Percent Favoring							
	No involvement		Discussion in sermon		Congregation as congregation		Church body officially	
Specific social issue	Laity	Clergy	Laity	Clergy	Laity	Clergy	Laity	Clergy
Church–government relationships	36	10	17	45	25	49	45	76
Education in schools	37	17	22	46	36	61	32	49
Rights of minorities	38	11	30	65	31	67	36	71
Substance abuse prevention	40	14	28	54	34	67	28	54
Equal treatment under the law	46	14	23	53	25	62	29	63
Medical-care issues	53	20	14	37	23	54	23	58
Handling of crime and criminals	55	21	23	47	18	50	18	52
Local zoning laws	67	33	5	15	24	52	4	8
Business–government relationship	73	38	8	26	10	31	11	42
Elections and candidates	75	50	8	17	12	24	6	17

On these same four issues 83 to 90 percent of the clergy believe that some sort of church involvement is appropriate.

No matter what the issue, some seven to 10 percent of the laity, some 18 to 25 percent of the clergy, believe that is not enough for the members as individuals to be involved.

There are clear differences of opinion, however, on the ways in which the church should be involved. Clergy, for example, proportionately are two or three times more likely than laity to favor discussion of the issues in sermons, to involve the congregation as an organization, and to expect church body involvement in the issue.

Perhaps surprisingly, however, both clergy and laity agree as to which level of involvement they most prefer in dealing with the particular issue. Official church involvement is the strongest preference of both groups in dealing with:

- rights of minorities
- equal treatment under the law
- medical-care issues
- church–government relationships
- church–business relationships.

If there is to be any church involvement in the specific issue, both clergy and laity give their plurality preference to involvement by the congregation as an organization in:

- substance abuse prevention
- education in schools
- local zoning laws
- elections and candidates.

The only issue on which clergy and laity differ in their plurality preference is in the handling of crime and criminals. Clergy give greatest weight to official church body involvement. Laity prefer discussion of the issue in sermons.

Differences of opinion between men and women on these matters are minimal. Regional differences also are minimal, with two exceptions. Lutherans in the Northeast are more desirous than Lutherans elsewhere of official church body involvement in issues relating to rights of minorities and to medical care. Lutherans in the South are least interested, of all of the regions, in official church body involvement in issues relating to rights of minorities.

One generalization regarding age differences appears warranted. Whereas church involvement is acceptable to at least 45 percent of the laity, persons under age 55 are much more likely than those over 55 both to favor involvement in the issue and to expect official church involvement.

One further generalization appears warranted from the data as a whole. Lutheran laity support church involvement in issues that directly or potentially affect persons, families, schools, and the church corporately. They are not so ready, however, to see their church involved in issues that pertain to the operation of other community agencies or institutions. Clergy are much more ready than laity to deal with the total range of issues and to deal with them in a variety of ways.

Where People Turn in Crises

The church is an important, but not the only, resource to which Lutheran laity first would turn in times of crisis. Their family is the first resource to which the majority first would turn in the event of a close family death or of severe money problems.

Faced with severe marital problems, the largest number would first turn to their pastor. A family alcoholism or drug-abuse problem would cause them to turn first either to private counsel or to their pastor. If unemployment occurred, their first line of sought-after help would be a government agency.

Should an unwanted pregnancy occur, no clear consensus is apparent. The largest number would handle the situation on their own. Nearly as many, however, would turn to their family, to their pastor, or to private counsel. A similar situation of divided directions is apparent in confronting a crisis of paralysis or retardation. The family is the first refuge for some 30 percent. Between 16 and 20 percent, however, would turn first either to a government agency, to private counsel, or handle the situation on their own.

One consistent difference between clergy and laity is evident. Clergy are more likely than laity to turn to private counsel to help them should these problems strike them or their families. In the cases of money problems or unemployment they are more likely than laity to turn to friends for help.

Only a few differences show in responses by men and by women. Men are more likely than women to turn to the pastor in the event of severe marital problems or an unwanted pregnancy. Women are more likely than men to turn to their families in the event of unemployment or severe money problems. Further, women are more likely than men to turn to private counsel in the event of family alcoholism or drug abuse problems and the event of an unwanted pregnancy.

In terms of age groups, the over-55s turn most often to the pastor rather than to the family in the case of the death of a close family member. Youth (under 21) find their friends a major source of help more often than do members of any other age group for every crisis other than severe money problems.

Regional variations are minimal. Lutherans in the South turn more often to their pastor for help in cases of family alcoholism or drug abuse than do Lutherans in the other regions. They turn less often to government agencies for help in problems of unemployment or of paralysis/retardation than do their sisters and brothers elsewhere in the U.S.A.

Support for the Church

How does a Lutheran decide how much to give to the church? If one is a clergyman, the answer is simple: pledge a percentage of one's income. Over 80 percent make this choice.

For laity, the pattern is a mixed one. Some 30 percent choose a specific sum for the year, based upon the previous year's giving. Another 24 percent decide each week or each month what they can afford to give. Yet another 22 percent pledge a portion of their income. Smaller proportions of Lutherans give of what they have when they attend church (11%) or give as needs of the congregation arise (7%).

Those over 55 years of age are far more likely than their younger fellow members either to pledge a portion of their income or to give as congregational needs arise. Pledging a percent of one's income also is more prevalent in the West than elsewhere.

Attitudes and practices regarding pledging vary. A majority of Lutherans, notably among those over the age of 35 and those in the South and West, regard pledging as necessary. Whether they do so gladly is another matter. Among the clergy, 85 percent gladly make a pledge of financial support to their congregation. Among the laity, however, only a 52 percent majority of those aged 36-55 gladly pledges.

Pledging is least acceptable in the North Central region, where only 40 percent gladly make this commitment to their congregation. One-fourth of the lay Lutherans in this region refuse to make a pledge of financial support to the church.

Only about 40 percent of Lutherans presently have a will. Even among those older than 55 only 58 percent have a will. The percentage of clergy with a will is similar, 59 percent.

Of those with a will, about 25 percent of the laity are leaving something to the church. The comparable ratio for the clergy is about 50 percent.

When those without written wills are asked if they would consider leaving something to the church when they have their wills written, some 60 percent indicate that they have never thought of the possibility. Some 20 percent, however, among both laity and clergy respond that they would not leave anything to the church in their wills. This attitude is strongest in the over-55 age group, 39 percent expressing this negative view.

The Congregations of Which They Are Members

Some data are available concerning the congregations in which survey respondents hold membership. These data may give some further meaning to data reported earlier in this chapter.

Roughly half of the congregations have over 500 members; the other half have 500 or fewer members. Around 60 percent of the congregations in the South and West have fewer than 501 members.

A comparison of the socioeconomic groups who make up at least 20 percent of the members of the congregation and at least 20 percent of the residents of the area close to the church shows this picture:

Socioeconomic group	Percent of Congregation	Percent of Residents
Middle income, managers, small farmers	85	72
Middle income, blue collar	76	70
Upper income, mid-level executives	52	39
Low income	28	31
Upper income, high status occupation	9	9
Poverty	1	7

Lutheran congregation members are more middle income, less low and poverty income than are the people who live around their church.

The programs and activities of these congregations include the following, with the percent of laity being members of congregations providing each indicated in parentheses:

Worship

evening, all year—(10%)
evening, all summer—(15%)
pan-Lutheran—(23%)
interfaith—(24%)

Educational

parochial school—(17%)

weekday school—(27%)

adult Bible class—(92%)

Evangelism

formal evangelism program—(44%)

regular worship broadcast—(11%)

other worship broadcasts—(9%)

Activities

adult choirs—(87%)

formal pledging done—(60%)

female officers of congregation—(76%)

Postscript

Again it appears that Lutheran laity see their congregation in "belonging to" terms. They look to it for "religious" rather than "social" purposes. In crises, except for severe marital problems, they turn first to resources other than the church. The financial support they give is based on what they think they can afford in relation to the needs demonstrated by the church. The meaning commitment implied in pledging a fixed percent of one's income is strong only among the clergy.

Leaders of Lutheran congregations and church bodies face a difficult question: how can Lutheran laity be helped to see that a congregation is not only for belonging to but also for finding meaning, purpose, and Christian commitment in the whole of life?

5

Involvement in the Community

Lutherans are selectively optimistic or pessimistic about the coming ten years, depending on the arena of life they are viewing. They seem only minimally involved in community issues and causes. Income production for men, home care for the women, are the leading ways in which they use their time. Lutherans, nevertheless, are organization members, belonging to a variety of church-affiliated, work-related, kindred support, community-involvement, recreational, and self-expression groups, sometimes two or more of a type. Different types of organizations, however, enlist different levels of participation, involvement, and satisfaction.

Attitudes Toward the Future

An important factor influencing involvement in the community is a person's feelings of optimism or pessimism about the coming ten years. About what areas of one's life does a person feel optimistic? What are the areas about which one feels pessimistic?

Lutherans are strongly optimistic about their own personal

future, their family relations, their congregation, and their church body. They are guardedly optimistic about their personal finances and about their country in the coming ten years. However, they more often are pessimistic than optimistic about the national economy and about world affairs. Men and women differ little in their feelings about these matters.

Age, however, makes a marked difference in how Lutherans feel about the nation and the world. Pessimism wanes, optimism waxes, after age 35 in appraising the national economy, the country, and world affairs. Even so, however, Lutherans of all ages are more pessimistic than optimistic about world affairs.

Two other age differences are quite understandable. Young adults, aged 21-35, are the most optimistic about their family relations. Older persons (over 55), though decidedly optimistic, are less optimistic than are younger persons about their own personal futures.

A few regional variations also are evident. By and large optimism is more restrained in the Northeast, more buoyant in the West, with respect to person, family, church, and economy. With respect to the country and to world affairs, regional variations are minimal.

Clergy are markedly more optimistic than are laity in their appraisal of their family relations and the local congregation. They are markedly more pessimistic than are the laity in their appraisal of the national economy, the country, and world affairs. In other areas their appraisals of the future are only minimally different from those of the laity.

Table 9 provides specifics for laity and clergy and for persons of four major age groups.

Involvement in Causes

Lutherans active in their church appear to be only minimally concerned about community issues and causes. Respondents

Table 9. Optimism or Pessimism About Coming Ten Years in Selected Areas of Life Among Laity and Clergy and Among Persons of Major Age Groups

			Percent of Group Expressing Optimism or Pessimism			
				Age groups		
	Laity	*Clergy*	*Under 21*	*21-35*	*36-55*	*Over 55*
Feelings About Coming Ten Years with Respect To:						
Personal future						
Optimism	80	81	83	88	84	74
Pessimism	5	3	3	3	5	6
Personal finance						
Optimism	59	56	57	65	62	57
Pessimism	16	18	16	15	17	14
Family relations						
Optimism	85	95	83	93	86	86
Pessimism	3	1	4	2	4	3
Local congregation						
Optimism	72	87	65	73	73	73
Pessimism	9	6	9	8	11	9
Church body						
Optimism	68	74	60	67	70	71
Pessimism	6	13	5	3	8	9
National economy						
Optimism	33	20	22	27	35	38
Pessimism	41	55	51	49	42	33
Country						
Optimism	58	37	37	54	62	60
Pessimism	25	45	34	30	26	19
World affairs						
Optimism	30	24	14	24	34	35
Pessimism	46	57	51	54	45	41

were asked to list local, state, and national "causes which you are concerned about." Their concerns include ten major areas:

Gun control—9%

School/education—9%

Government, political party—7%

Environment, pollution—6%

Civil rights protection—6%

Economy, inflation—5%

Crime control, law enforcement—5%

ERA—5%

Taxes—5%

Hospital, hospital auxiliary—5%

The fact that only from five to nine percent indicate any of these areas as being of concern to them suggests only a minimal depth of commitment. This is substantiated by the fact that only among those concerned about hospitals and their auxiliaries are the majority active in that cause. This cause involves particularly the women. Men are most concerned about gun control.

School and education matters concern about one in eight persons within the ages of 28 and 55. A similar ratio of clergy expresses concern about school matters. The majority both among clergy and among persons 36-55 years of age take active roles in education causes.

Clergy also are concerned about governmental and political party matters almost twice as often as are the laity. The majority of the clergy concerned about this area are active in the cause.

Uses of Time

Income production for the men, home care for the women, are the leading ways in which Lutheran adults use their time.

For both men and women such personal activities as reading, television viewing, hobbies, and social events or activities take up the second largest segment of their time. Volunteer services in church and community, which involve less than 60 percent of either men or women, are in last place among major ways in which Lutheran respondents use their time.

Transit time to and from work, church, meetings, etc., is in third place for men, in fourth place for women. Income production is the third largest time-use factor for the women respondents.

Differences between clergy and male laity in the allocations of their time are marked. This shows particularly in the percentage of time devoted by clergy to income production, in sacrifice of time given to home care and to personal activities.

The following table shows the average percent of time devoted by laymen, laywomen, and clergy to:

	Income Production	Home Care	Personal Activities	Transit	Volunteer Services
Laymen	33	17	24	20	6
Laywomen	19	36	21	17	7
Clergy	49	12	17	15	7

Nearly half of the youth give over 40 percent of their time to personal activities and to transit. Less than half of those over 55 engage either in income production or in volunteer services.

Types of Groups with Which Affiliated

Lutherans indeed are members of a wide variety of groups. Less than one in five (18%) is not a member of any group or organization. In the West only about one in eight (13%) is not a member of some group, organization, or association. Among the clergy, only one in twenty (5%) is not a member of some such group.

Typically, one half of all Lutherans are members of some church-affiliated group. Around 20 percent are members either of a sports group (22%) or of a professional organization (20%). Around 15 percent are members of a service club (16%) or of a school service group (15%).

Far in the lead, then, are church-related groups. Secondary in importance are sports, professional, and service groups. Others which attract more than 10 percent of Lutherans into their membership are fraternal, youth, senior citizens, study, and self-improvement groups. Relatively in fourth rank are such organizations as hobby clubs, labor unions, farm organizations, political parties, social-action groups, veterans organizations, and performing-arts groups. Each of these attracts from six to 10 percent of Lutherans into membership. Only one in 50 Lutherans is a member of an organization built around ethnic-group heritage.

When organizations are grouped into categories which serve essentially similar purposes, a different pattern is evident. Church-affiliated groups remain the ones involving the majority of Lutherans. Two other major categories of organizations, however, involve nearly as large a proportion of Lutherans as members as do the church groups. One of these includes groups which center around involvement in community life. The other includes groups which provide mutual support of persons in kindred life-experience situations. (Refer to Table 10 for specifics.)

Closely grouped are three categories of organizations which enroll about one-third of the laity. These are the work-related groups (37%), the recreational groups (32%), and the self-expression groups (32%). In each of the six categories of groups except for the recreational, clergy are members in consistently higher ratio than are the laity.

Proportionately twice as many men as women are members of work-related groups; virtually twice as many women as men are members of self-expression groups. In the "kindred support" groups, men are more often members of veterans and fraternal groups; women, of personal support groups. In the community involvement category, men are more often members of political groups; women, of school service clubs.

As would be expected, clergy are much more likely than laity to be involved in groups which are either church-related, professional, youth, service, social-action, or study-oriented. They are less likely to be members of a labor union.

Membership in church-affiliated groups is highest in the

Table 10. Types of Organizations of Which Laity and Clergy Are Members

Type of Organization	Percent of Respondents Who Are Members of Type of Organization				Percent of Members Who Are Members of Two or More of Type			
	Laity	Male	Female	Clergy	Laity	Male	Female	Clergy
Church-affiliated groups	53	51	56	86	41	38	45	63
Work-related groups								
Labor union	10	15	5	1	7	5	3	0
Farm organization	7	10	6	3	28	26	29	11
Professional association	20	27	15	62	29	32	24	35
Kindred support groups								
Veterans club	7	11	4	5	20	24	11	17
Fraternal group	12	15	10	15	18	22	13	12
Ethnic group	2	2	2	5	7	9	6	8
Youth group	13	14	14	39	18	23	14	21
Senior citizen group	10	9	10	14	17	24	12	6
Personal-support group	6	3	8	13	12	21	10	12
Community involvement								
Service clubs	16	16	16	32	19	16	22	12
Political group	8	11	6	14	8	5	9	7
Social-action group	9	8	10	25	22	17	24	17
School service club	15	10	19	20	19	18	18	13
Recreational								
Sports group	22	27	19	23	30	32	28	19
Hobby club	10	9	10	7	19	28	13	9
Self-expression								
Literary, discussion study groups	11	8	13	27	13	12	12	22
Self-improvement	13	7	17	10	14	9	15	10
Performing arts	7	5	8	8	24	35	22	10

36-55 age group, where 61 percent are members. Only 42 percent of the youth (under 21) and 45 percent of the young adults (21-35) are members of church-affiliated groups.

Youth, for their part, are notable for their membership not only in youth groups but also in school service clubs, sports groups, hobby clubs, and performing-arts groups.

Persons aged 21-55, the years of prime employment, naturally are far above average in membership in professional associations. Members of veterans organizations are mostly in the 45-55 age range. Older persons show tendencies to decreasing their memberships, not only in work-related, community-involvement, recreational, and self-expression categories of groups but also in church-affiliated groups. Their involvement partially is transferred to senior citizen groups. And, sports groups involve decreasing percentages of persons as age advances—39 percent of the youth, 14 percent of those over 55.

Regionally, a few variations appear. Northeast Lutherans less often are members of church-affiliated groups, professional associations, or study groups. North Central Lutherans more often are members of farm organizations. Lutherans in the South are above average in their membership in professional associations and lowest in labor-union membership. Lutherans in the West have the highest percentage of membership in church-affiliated groups and in sports groups.

Dual Membership in Types of Organizations

Certain types of organizations are so important to some persons that they become members of two or more groups of that type. For example, about 40 percent of the laity and about 60 percent of the clergy who are members of church-affiliated groups are members of two or more church-affiliated groups. (Refer again to Table 10.)

Other types in which at least one-fourth of the laity are members of two or more groups are sports groups, professional associations, farm organizations, and performing-arts groups.

Clergy tend to concentrate their dual memberships only in their professional associations, 35 percent holding membership in two or more.

More often than women, men tend to hold dual memberships in work-related, kindred support, and recreational groups. Women, in turn, more often than men are members of two or more church-related and of community-involvement groups.

Age and regional comparisons reveal no distinctive patterns.

Levels of Involvement

Two measures of organizational involvement are available. One indicates the organizations to which one devotes the largest amount of time. The other indicates whether one is a leader, an active worker, a regular or an occasional participant in the organization.

Only two types of groups of which they are members claim a significant investment of the time of Lutherans. In first place are church-affiliated groups, to which 28 percent of the laity and 61 percent of the clergy members give the most organizational time. In far distant second place are sports groups for the laity and professional associations for the clergy. Only about 10 percent of laity and clergy give the largest block of their organizational-membership time to groups of these types.

Similar patterns hold for both men and women. Age variations are evident. Youth under 21 gave the largest amount of their organizational time to sports groups. For young adults (21-35) sports groups closely rival church groups in their time commitments. For persons over the age of 35, at least one-third give their major time commitment to church groups.

Different types of organizations enlist different levels of participation. A person may be a leader in one type, an active worker in another, a regular participant in a third, and participate only occasionally in a fourth. Men and women also participate at different levels of activity in the different types of organizations of which they are members. Table 11 provides data for three levels of organizational activity by men and women.

Table 11. Levels of Activity of Men and Women in Organization

| | Percent of members who are | | | | | |
| | Leader or Active Workers | | Regular Participant | | Occasional Participant | |
Types of organizations	Men	Women	Men	Women	Men	Women
Church-affiliated groups	59	66	31	26	8	7
Work-related groups						
Labor union	29	20	26	63	43	17
Farm organization	29	13	28	70	22	17
Professional association	52	40	33	37	14	23
Kindred support groups						
Veterans club	26	54	18	22	49	17
Fraternal group	36	39	12	42	47	13
Ethnic group	51	90	44	10	5	0
Youth group	91	72	1	16	8	12
Senior citizen group	48	37	17	44	35	18
Personal-support group	54	29	32	48	14	23
Community involvement						
Service clubs	58	69	24	12	18	19
Political group	31	62	5	26	60	2
Social-action group	74	55	21	41	5	4
School service club	80	75	13	20	6	5
Recreational						
Sports group	27	14	57	76	16	9
Hobby club	26	17	25	62	49	15
Self-expression						
Literary, discussion study groups	9	15	75	76	6	9
Self-improvement	19	20	58	74	23	6
Performing arts	40	43	60	56	0	1

Note: The difference between the total level of activity for each group and 100 is the percent of members not answering this item.

It will be noted that both youth groups and school service groups involve upwards of 70 percent of both men and women members in leadership or active-worker roles. Church-affiliated groups and service clubs involve upwards of around 60 percent of both men and women in leadership or active-worker roles.

The only other types of organizations in which a majority of both men and women members are active as leaders or workers are the few ethnic groups and the larger number of social-action groups. The performing-arts and the fraternal groups involve around 40 percent of both men and women in major roles.

More often than women, men tend to be the leaders or active workers in the many types of organizations. The exceptions among the groups involving large numbers of members are church-affiliated groups and service clubs. Among groups having lesser numbers of members, women proportionately are more actively involved than men in veterans, ethnic, political, and study groups.

Rarely do women members rate themselves as "only occasional" participants. In no type of organization do as many as 25 percent of the women so regard themselves. Among men, however, at least 40 percent rate themselves as "only occasional" participants in labor unions, veterans clubs, fraternal groups, political groups, and hobby clubs. Rarely do persons who are members of a church group, an ethnic group, a social-action group, a school service club, a study group, or a performing-arts group regard themselves as "only occasional" participants in its work. This is true for both men and women.

Interestingly, the majority of both the men and women who are members of sports, study, self-improvement, and performing-arts groups regard themselves as "regular participants." The implication is clear that persons become members of recreational and self-expression groups for the satisfaction they find inhering in these activities rather than for gaining leadership recognition.

Age and regional differences are inconclusive. Clergy, when

members, are much more likely than laity to be heavily involved as either leaders or active workers. The only exceptions are ethnic groups, personal-support groups, social-action groups, and performing-arts groups.

Reasons for Participating

As different organizations enlist different degrees of member participation, so members have different reasons for participating in the different organizations.

By and large, persons are moved to participate in work-related organizations either because they feel an obligation to do so or because they want to support the cause.

The same is true of membership in political groups. In each instance between 48 and 62 percent give these as the strongest reasons for their participation.

One-half of the participants in church-affiliated groups and in service clubs do so because of their satisfaction that their volunteer service is needed.

Another pattern is dominant for sports groups, hobby clubs, self-improvement groups, and performing-arts groups. Here, for both laity and clergy, participation primarily is because of the enjoyment or fun it provides.

Detailed data are provided in Table 12. Variations in responses of men and women exhibit no clear patterns of differences. Not shown in the table is an interesting sidelight. At least one in every five members of study and discussion, personal-support, and self-improvement groups add "other" reasons for their participation. These include health, religious, and personal-improvement considerations.

Levels of Interest and Satisfaction

Higher proportions of women than of men express "great interest" in the organizations of which they are members. Except for veterans clubs, service clubs, and hobby clubs, a clear

Table 12. Major Reasons for Participation in Various Organizations as Given by Laity and Clergy

Types of Organizations	Feeling of Obligation, to Support the Cause		Satisfaction That Volunteer Service Is Needed		Enjoyment, Fun	
	Laity	*Clergy*	*Laity*	*Clergy*	*Laity*	*Clergy*
Church-affiliated groups	30	51	49	22	15	7
Work-related groups						
Labor union	62	0	9	0	10	0
Farm organization	48	0	8	0	2	0
Professional association	49	47	17	26	12	9
Kindred support groups						
Veterans club	29	63	30	0	23	0
Fraternal group	25	0	30	0	44	100
Ethnic group	12	100	17	0	69	0
Youth group	10	32	37	56	28	0
Senior-citizen group	16	21	30	79	39	0
Personal-support group	11	0	16	38	25	12
Community involvement						
Service clubs	28	20	50	49	20	9
Poiltical group	61	77	32	23	8	0
Social-action group	29	54	36	43	37	0
School service club	31	62	33	24	28	0
Recreational						
Sports group	3	0	3	17	84	62
Hobby club	20	19	11	0	93	81
Self-expression						
Literary, discussion study groups	8	17	18	45	41	11
Self-improvement	7	0	7	22	72	54
Performing arts	15	0	12	8	68	92

majority of the women express "great interest" in all of the church-affiliated, kindred support, community-involvement, recreational, and self-expression types of groups.

The only types of organizations for which men more often than women express "great interest" are two of the three work-related groups, personal-support groups, and hobby clubs. Indeed, less than one-third of the men show "great interest" in any of the work-related groups. Their interest in political

Table 13. Percent of Respondents Expressing Great Interest, Great Satisfaction in Participation in Various Types of Organizations

Types of Organizations	Great Interest				Great Satisfaction			
	Laity 57	Clergy 63	Men 44	Women 66	Laity 57	Clergy 49	Men 48	Women 64
Church-affiliated groups								
Work-related groups								
Labor union	27	0	18	52	16	0	14	36
Farm organization	29	0	27	14	25	0	20	14
Professional association	31	39	32	25	23	26	25	18
Kindred support groups								
Veterans club	37	61	37	36	35	37	28	42
Fraternal group	42	0	37	54	45	100	43	51
Ethnic group	94	100	85	99	98	100	95	99
Youth group	54	40	52	56	50	40	47	53
Senior-citizen group	36	71	12	53	41	100	17	60
Personal-support group	75	52	78	72	76	31	62	81
Community involvement								
Service clubs	42	18	40	48	48	26	46	54
Political group	52	61	18	80	48	61	14	78
Social-action group	57	17	55	61	32	15	19	42
School service club	55	30	50	58	46	28	57	44
Recreational								
Sports group	51	46	45	54	58	64	55	60
Hobby club	44	42	53	38	53	62	60	49
Self-expression								
Literary, discussion study groups	70	48	78	73	70	47	83	70
Self-improvement	49	20	36	55	55	41	52	62
Performing arts	71	92	66	73	63	92	75	60

groups and in senior-citizen organizations is at an even lower level. (See Table 13 for substantiating detail.)

As pointed out earlier, there are five types of organizations (church, professional, sports, community service, and school service) in which at least 15 percent of the laity are members. Of these five, clergy express great interest more often than laity only in their church-affiliated groups and in their professional associations. Evident differences for other types of organizations often are skewed by the small numbers of cases involved.

A comparison of organizations in which persons express "great interest" and those from which they derive "great satisfaction" offers an interesting picture. (Refer again to Table 13.) Both men and women more often are greatly satisfied by their participation in hobby and self-improvement groups than basically are interested in the groups *per se*.

Men express great satisfaction more often than great interest in the ethnic, school service, sports, and peforming-arts groups. Women find senior-citizen and personal-support groups providing greater satisfaction than their level of interest would suggest.

Noteworthy is the fact that a majority, or near majority, of both men and women gain great satisfaction from their participation in church-affiliated, ethnic, youth, personal-support, and service organizations. Moreover, they find great satisfaction in each of the recreational and self-expression types of groups.

Postscript

There is little doubt that committed Lutherans are interested in and active in their church-affiliated organizations. Similarly, they are interested in and active in organizations relating to youth and to schools. Further, they are interested in and active in organizations which foster their own personal relaxation and/or personal development and self-expression.

Apart from service groups and school service organizations, Lutherans are only minimally involved in their communities. Though they join work-related groups in large numbers, they do so more out of obligation than for personal satisfaction.

Is Lutheran pessimism about the nation's economy and about world affairs a deterrent to Lutheran involvement in civic affairs? Does the pessimism of the clergy, which includes the future of the country as well as the nation's economy and world affairs in its negative grasp, communicate itself to the laity? Is this Lutheran pessimism perhaps rooted in a distorted understanding of the depravity of that world beyond self, family, and church?

If a change is to be made, perhaps it will be through conscious theological development of emphases inherent in the Lutheran Confessions. Lutherans have a long tradition of support of educational and welfare causes under church auspices. Lutherans have a high regard for their church. If their church now, with clear theological groundings, would encourage at least some of its affiliated agencies and groups to address themselves to community issues and causes, most members of the congregations would respect that encouragement.

Lutherans honor the Scriptures. Lutherans understand the parable of the good Samaritan (Luke 10:29-37). What they need to see is that community action to make the highway of life safe for travel also is part of their opportunity to prove themselves neighborly.

6

Household Income
and Giving Patterns

Lutheran households typically include spouse and children. Household income in 1980 averaged about $20,000 for the year, with some regional and family life-cycle differences. Men are more likely than women to be the sole income earners. Contributions to the church divide at the ten dollars a week level, half of the households above, half below, this amount. Voluntary contributions to other causes, whether church-related or community, are at a far lower level.

Composition of the Households

Respondents provided data on the households in which they live. From these data it appears that four out of five live in families where both a husband and a wife are present. In just about one-third of the families (31%) there are children 13 years of age or younger, and in about one-third (33%) there are children 14 and older living in the family. In each instance one or two children 13 or younger, 14 or older, are characteristic.

One in five of the respondents is single. Among these single persons are the three percent of all respondents who are single parents. Single persons are proportionately twice as numerous among the women as among the men—23 percent and 12 percent. Nearly nine of every ten men (88%) live in husband-and-wife households.

As would be expected, respondents aged 21-35 most often (62%) had children in the 13 and younger ages; respondents aged 36-55 most often (60%) had children 14 and older living at home.

Total Household Income

The typical Lutheran family appears to have had a 1980 total income of around $20,000. Exactly 50 percent report an income of at least $20,000, 44 percent an income of under $20,000, and six percent give no information on this income.

With incomes grouped another way, major one-thirds appear. One-third of the laity had incomes of at least $25,000, one-third in the $15-25,000 range, the other one-third having less than $15,000 or giving no income information.

Clergy families proportionately more often than laity have total incomes in the $10,000 to $30,000 range. Less often than the laity, clergy have incomes either of under $10,000 or over $30,000.

Compared with 1979 U.S. family incomes, Lutheran families equal their share of over $25,000 incomes, exceed the U.S. average in the proportions with incomes in the $15,000 to $25,000 range, and fall below the U.S. proportions with incomes of less than $10,000.

In terms of the Lutheran population alone, families with youth under 21 and also middle-age families (36-55) most often have total incomes of over $25,000 (40 and 50 percent, respectively). Persons in the young-adult bracket most often fall into the $15,000 to $25,000 income range, as do the clergy (48 and 46 percent respectively). Persons over 55, however, most often have incomes of less than $15,000 (45%).

Regionally, Lutherans in the Northeast most often have in-

comes in the $15,000 to $25,000 range (39%). Those in the
North Central divide almost evenly among the under $15,000,
the $15,000 to $25,000, and the over $25,000 brackets in their
household income. About two of every five Lutherans in the
South and West have incomes upwards of $25,000. In each
region from three to six percent give no income data.

Income bracket data for clergy and laity, and for Lutherans
in the four regions, appear in Table 14.

Table 14. Household Incomes, 1980, Laity and Clergy, and in Four Regions

			Percent of Group in Specific Income Bracket			
	Laity	Clergy	North-east	North Central	South	West
Income bracket						
Under $10,000	13	6	11	15	11	13
$10,000-$14,999	14	24	14	15	15	12
$15,000-$19,999	17	23	19	18	15	13
$20,000-$24,999	16	23	20	15	15	18
$25,000-$29,000	10	13	9	11	9	11
$30,000-$34,999	9	7	9	8	11	10
$35,000 and over	15	4	12	13	21	19
No answer	6	0	6	5	3	4

Contributors to Household Income

Twice as many men as women, proportionately—40 and 19
percent, respectively—are the sole contributors of the household income. When men are not the sole wage earners, their
earnings account for upwards of 60 percent of the total household income. Some 30 percent of the women earn no income.
When women are wage earners, the share they add to the
household income is largely in the 20 to 60 percent range.

Clergy also are the major contributors to their household
incomes. For 45 percent, theirs is the sole family income. For
another 49 percent, the clergy earnings amount to upwards
of 60 percent of the family income.

Regional variations are minimal. Variations among age

groups offer few surprises. Youth are primarily noncontributors to the family income. Among the young adults and the middle-aged, the influence of several wage earners in the family is evident. Among the over-55s, however, a larger than average percent of persons are the sole provider and fewer than average are noncontributors.

When all members of the households are considered, regardless of age, 64 percent of the males, 46 percent of the females, make some contribution to the household income. Males are likely to be the sole contributors to, or contributors of the majority of the total income of the household. When women members add their earnings to the "household pot," their share is rarely above the 60 percent level.

Again, regional variations are minimal. By ages, the variations are expected. Over 90 percent of those under 21 and 31 percent of those 21-35 make no income contribution. Those over 55 years of age have the highest percent of sole contributors and the lowest percent of noncontributors. Among those 36-55 years of age, percent contributions to the family income are fairly evenly spaced along the percentage spectrum.

Financial Support for Congregation

About one-half (49%) of Lutheran laity households contribute less than ten dollars per week to their congregations. About one-half (47%) contribute ten dollars or more.

About three-fourths (76%) of Lutheran clergy households contribute more than twenty dollars per week, as many as 42 percent more than thirty dollars per week, to their congregation.

So marked are laity–clergy differences in their financial contributions to their own congregation! The data on contributions compared with income permit a pertinent deduction. Laity appear to contribute about 2.6 percent of their income to the church, clergy over 7.0 percent.

The following table shows the percent of respondents in

major age groups from whose households specified amounts per week are contributed to their congregation:

Amount Per Week	Under 21	21-35	36-55	Over 55
Under $5.00	31	39	19	17
$5.00-$9.00	19	24	25	22
$10.00-$19.99	16	21	31	33
$20.00-$29.99	16	8	14	14
$30.00 and over	11	6	11	13
No answer	7	2	0	1

Note that for those under 36, the most common amount is in the under $5.00 bracket; for those over 35, the most common amount is in the $10 to $20 range. The stage at which the person or the household is on the family life-cycle is a significant factor influencing giving patterns.

Regionally, a 55 percent majority of Lutheran households in the Northeast contribute less than $10 per week to their congregation. In the South and West, however, about 55 percent majority contribute $10 or more per week. Indeed, at least 25 percent in these two regions contribute upwards of $20 per week.

Giving to Other Causes

Lutheran laity by and large do not contribute significantly to organizations and causes beyond the congregation. Only the United Fund and "other charities" and causes special to the contributors draw support from over half of the Lutheran households. Even in these two instances just under one-half of the contributors to the former and somewhat over one-half to the latter, make their gift in an amount upwards of $20.

A second tier of causes draws support from 41 to 46 percent of the households. These causes include Lutheran social-service agencies and institutions and the various medical charities. In around 60 percent of the cases the contribution is less than $20.

A third tier of causes draws support from around one in four Lutheran households—22 to 28 percent. These organizations include religious non-Lutheran causes (22%), Lutheran schools and colleges (25%), and national Lutheran programs (28%). In around 55 percent of the cases the gift is under $20.

Far down the line are two types of programs which draw support from only around 15 percent of the households. These include non-Lutheran educational institutions and Lutheran radio and television programming. In the case of the former about half of the gifts are under $20. Support for Lutheran broadcasting is greater, 60 percent of the gifts being upwards of $20.

Marked differences occur in the contribution patterns of young-adult households and those of older persons. (See Table 15 for specific details.) Generally, older households contribute in higher ratio and in larger amounts. Exceptions to the ratio pattern are evident in support given to non-Lutheran educational institutions, to "other charities," and to medical charities. In the case of the first two, there are no ratio differences. In the

Table 15. Household Non-Congregational Contribution Patterns, Laity and Clergy, Respondents Aged 21-35 and Over 55

	Percent Contributing, Percent of Contributors Making Gift of Amount Indicated			
Cause and Contributor Pattern	*Laity*	*Clergy*	*Age 21-35*	*Age over 55*
National Lutheran programs				
Percent who contribute	**28**	**62**	**20**	**38**
Under $20	54	24	67	53
$20-$50	25	34	19	22
Over $50	21	42	14	25
Lutheran social service				
Percent who contribute	**41**	**67**	**33**	**51**
Under $20	59	42	71	51
$20-$50	28	38	23	34
Over $50	13	20	6	15

Table 15 — *Continued*

Percent Contributing, Percent of Contributors Making Gift of Amount Indicated

Cause and Contributor Pattern	Laity	Clergy	Age 21-35	Age over 55
Lutheran schools and colleges				
Percent who contribute	25	65	19	31
Under $20	52	28	63	47
$20-$50	21	29	17	23
Over $50	27	43	20	30
Lutheran radio, TV programs				
Percent who contribute	14	30	10	21
Under $20	40	22	42	46
$20-$50	40	50	39	26
Over $50	20	28	19	28
Non-Lutheran educ. institutions				
Percent who contribute	15	17	15	15
Under $20	51	46	61	45
$20-$50	27	35	16	36
Over $50	22	19	23	19
Non-Lutheran religious causes				
Percent who contribute	22	35	17	27
Under $20	57	48	55	61
$20-$50	22	31	23	18
Over $50	21	21	22	21
United Fund				
Percent who contribute	55	56	56	67
Under $20	51	54	58	51
$20-$50	26	32	25	31
Over $50	23	14	17	18
Medical charities				
Percent who contribute	46	43	50	43
Under $20	61	69	70	56
$20-$50	27	22	24	31
Over $50	12	9	6	13
Other charities, causes				
Percent who contribute	58	62	60	59
Under $20	45	38	56	39
$20-$50	29	33	29	28
Over $50	26	29	15	33

case of the latter, young adults support medical charities in higher ratio than do older-person households. Further, the young adults are somewhat more generous in support of non-Lutheran religious causes than are their elders.

Regionally, only the Northeast shows deviations from the basic patterns evident in the other three regions. Proportionately Northeast Lutheran households contribute least often in support of national Lutheran causes, Lutheran schools and colleges, non-Lutheran religious causes, and Lutheran radio and television programming. They are far in the lead, however, in their ratio support for medical charities.

Clergy–laity differences are significant in several areas. Clergy are much more likely than laity, for example, to contribute to national Lutheran programs, Lutheran social-service agencies, Lutheran schools and colleges, Lutheran radio and television programming, and non-Lutheran religious causes. Their gifts, too, are likely to be significantly larger. (Refer again to Table 15.)

Contribution ratios between clergy and laity differ little in support of non-Lutheran causes generally, including educational institutions, United Fund, medical charities, and other charities. Indeed, for medical charities, clergy giving ratios are lower than those of the laity.

Postscript

This chapter touches on the pocketbook nerve, perhaps the most sensitive nerve in the human system. Lutheran laity are not poor. Yet, by and large, they are not generous in their financial contributions either to the church or to causes and organizations in the community.

Two questions seem pertinent. What is it that causes the clergy, near the average in income, to be so much more generous in their giving to the church and to Lutheran causes generally? How can their vision and their sense of commitment be communicated as an inspiration and an example for the laity to follow?

7

Residence and Mobility

Lutherans are largely a Northern, small-city and rural-area body of people. As are most young folk, their young are the most likely to move, though not necessarily for long distances. Impelling most moves are work, neighborhood, and family reasons. Of the many adjustments movement to a new community requires, most are made quickly. Clergy are considerably more likely to move than are the laity.

Regions and States

Though they can be found in every state of the nation, Lutherans are concentrated primarily in the North Central states. Some 32 percent live in the five Great Lakes states— Ohio, Michigan, Indiana, Illinois, and Wisconsin. Another 29 percent live in the seven Northern Plains states of Minnesota, North and South Dakota, Iowa, Missouri, Nebraska, and Kansas.

By contrast, only 18 percent of the nation's population lives in the Great Lakes states and only eight percent in the Northern Plains states. Thus, some 61 percent of the Lutherans in the U.S.A., but 26 percent of the nation's total population, live in these twelve North Central states.

Lutherans are particularly underrepresented in the South and the West. Some 33 percent of the nation's people live in the South and another 19 percent in the West. Among Lutherans, however, only 12 percent live in the South, 11 percent in the West.

There are two portions of the United States where Lutheran distribution is not far different from the total population distribution. One is the Middle Atlantic area of New York, New Jersey, and Pennsylvania. The other is the tier of Rocky Mountain states extending southward from Montana and Idaho.

All told, Lutherans reside especially in the northern portion of the United States, 80 percent of them in these 15 states:

New York	Wisconsin	North Dakota
Pennsylvania	Illinois	Nebraska
Ohio	Minnesota	Texas
Michigan	Iowa	Washington
Indiana	Missouri	California

Only two of these 15 are "sunbelt" states. Except for Washington and perhaps Missouri, all of the others are part of what often is termed the "frostbelt."

Between 1970 and 1980 the balance of the nation's population shifted from the Northeast and North Central states to the South and West. In 1970, 52 percent of the population lived in the Northeastern and North Central states. In 1980, 52 percent of the population lived in the Southern and Western states. Lutheran membership distribution remained unchanged: 77 percent in the Northeast and North Central states, 23 percent in the Southern and Western states.

Size of Community

The majority of Lutherans (57%) live in small cities of less than 50,000 population, in small towns and villages, and in the open country. Barely over one-fourth (27%) live in cities of over 250,000 population, including their suburbs. Virtually as many (26%) live in rural areas, including towns of less than 2500 residents and the open country.

Lutherans in the South and West, however, are urban dwellers. About 60 percent in these two regions live in cities having upwards of 50,000 residents. Indeed, 36 percent live in metropolitan areas of over 250,000 population. In contrast, only 34 percent of the North Central Lutherans live in cities having upwards of 50,000 residents.

An interesting sidelight relates to the residence of men and women. Proportionately more men than women live in rural areas under 2500 population, 30 and 23 percent respectively. Proportionately more women than men, however, reside both in towns of 2500 to 10,000 population and in large cities of 250,000 to 1,000,000 population. These two sizes of communities together are the residence for 35 percent of the women, 26 percent of the men.

Migration patterns during the past five years have accentuated this small city, rural residency among Lutherans. Of those who moved, 50 percent five years earlier lived in urban areas upwards of 50,000 population; 34 percent lived in places of less than 10,000 population.

Table 16 provides a more detailed summary of these residential patterns. Included are data for clergy. They too joined in the movement to rural areas and out of major metropolitan areas.

Frequency of Mobility

Moving from one residence to another is a common experience for young adults aged 21-35. Eighty percent of this young

Table 16. Comparison of Size of Community of Residence, Present and Five Years Ago for Those Who Moved, for Laity and Clergy, Male and Female Laity

Size of Community	Total	Percent in Present Size of Community			Percent of Those Who Moved by Size of Community 5 Years Ago			
		Laity Male	Female	Clergy Total	Total	Laity Male	Female	Clergy Total
Major metropolitan and suburbs (1,000,000 and over)	11	12	11	15	16	17	14	21
Large city and suburbs (250,000 to 1,000,000)	16	14	18	13	15	15	16	14
Medium city and suburbs (50,000 to 250,000)	16	16	15	13	19	20	19	14
Small city (10,000 to 50,000)	16	16	16	17	16	18	16	17
Town (2500 to 10,000)	15	12	17	13	13	12	12	13
Rural areas Town or village	11	12	9	19	9	9	9	16
Open country	15	18	14	10	12	9	14	5
Total, all sizes	100	100	100	100	100	100	100	100

group of Lutherans no longer lives in the same residence they lived in five years earlier. In contrast, 78 percent of older persons over 55 years of age still live in the same residence as five years earlier.

Western Lutherans also are somewhat more likely to have moved than are their Northeastern fellow members, 39 percent to 31 percent.

Taking a longer time interval—ten years—as many as 42 percent of the laity have not changed residence over the past ten years. But, less than ten percent of those laity within the ages of 21 to 35, and less than 20 percent of the clergy, are still living in their residence of ten years earlier. In contrast, well over half of those persons 45 and older continue residing where they had been ten years earlier.

Clearly, residential mobility involves young adults and the clergy far more directly than it does the middle-aged and older. Table 17 provides pertinent details.

Table 17 also shows how much more frequently the young persons move than do their elders. Note that one-fourth of those young adults 21-35 move five times or more, and that nearly 60 percent move at least three times in ten years. Clergy too are likely to move more often than are the laity.

By regions, Lutherans in the Northeast appear somewhat more rooted than do those in the other regions. Almost one-half (49%) did not change residence during the decade. Yet, if those living there did move, they more often made two to four moves than did Lutherans in the other regions.

The effects of these differing mobility patterns show up another way in the respondents' number of years in their present residence. Nearly two-thirds (63%) of the young adults (21-35) have lived in their present residence less than five years. An equal percent (63%) of those over 55 have lived in their present residence 15 years or more. Over half of the clergy have been in their present residence less than five years, a total of 80 percent less than ten years.

Table 17. Mobility Patterns by Groups of Respondents Over Past 10 Years

Group of Respondents	Percent Not Moving in 10 Years	Percent of Those Who Moved, by Number of Moves Made			
		One	Two	Three or Four	Five or More
Laity					
Total	42	44	19	22	15
Male	42	46	15	22	17
Female	41	41	22	23	14
Age					
Under 21	22	52	13	22	13
21-27	6	22	20	31	27
28-35	8	22	20	32	26
36-44	43	45	25	23	7
45-55	56	65	13	15	7
Over 55	62	70	20	8	2
Region					
Northeast	49	35	24	28	13
North Central	41	48	18	20	14
South	39	42	16	25	17
West	38	35	22	26	17
Clergy	18	31	22	27	20

Regionally, the majority of Lutherans in the South and West have lived in their present residence less than ten years. In the Northeast and North Central, the majority have lived in their present residence for more than ten years.

Though mobility is common for the young laity, the distance between previous and present residence is not over five miles for 40 percent of the young adults who moved. Among the clergy, however, the move crosses over 100 miles for two-thirds of those who made a change in residence. Moves of over 100 miles from the previous to the present residence are more common in the South and West (42% of all moves) than in the Northeast or North Central. In these latter two regions one-third move over 100 miles.

Changes with Mobility

Lutherans move, no doubt, for reasons similar to those of their neighbors. About 25 percent move for job-related reasons, another 25 percent because of factors related to home and neighborhood, another about 20 percent for family-related reasons. Health and quality-of-life factors influence another 15 percent.

Among clergy, moves take place almost entirely because of occupational opportunities related to their calling. Corresponding work-related factors also are the largest factor impelling mobility among laity between 28 and 55 years of age, particularly among those who are 45 to 55. For those under 28, family-related reasons are the factor most often mentioned.

Men are somewhat more likely than women, 31 to 24 percent, to move for work-related reasons. Women, for their part, are somewhat more likely than men, 23 to 17 percent, to move for family-related reasons. Health and quality-of-life factors influence some 20 percent of the moves to the South and West, considerably more than to any other region.

Major changes come with mobility. The majority of Lutherans (56%) undergo a change in the size of their dwelling. Around one-third experience a change between ownership and rental (35%) and a change in the size of the community in which they now live (32%). Somewhat over one-fourth (27%) experience a change in their work, including transition to retirement.

Though the precise percentages vary somewhat, these four changes—in size of dwelling, ownership or tenancy, size of community, and in work—consistently are the leading changes associated with mobility of Lutherans. They prevail for men and women, in each region and in all age groups except the youth (under 21). For youth, changes in proximity to school and to church are more frequent than changes in home ownership or in work.

Important, but secondary, changes come in proximity to

work or school (21%), to family and friends (19%), and to church (17%). For young adults 21-35, proximity to work and proximity to family and friends are virtually equal in importance with changes in employment. Each is a factor for one-fourth of those who experience changes with their move to their current residence.

Clergy, more acutely than laity, experience changes in their work (77%) and in the size of the community (68%). They closely parallel the laity in their experience with a home of a different size (55%) and in home-ownership status (31%). Clergy underscore more than do the laity the changes experienced in proximity to family and friends (35%) and to the church (34%).

Time Needed to Adjust

Depending on the distance moved, a change in residence may require many changes or none at all. The move may occasion the need to find a new physician, to change banks, to register as a voter, to transfer one's membership to a new congregation, to make both nonwork acquaintances and new friends, and to feel "at home" in the new place. The changes may take weeks, or even months, to complete.

The majority of the laity do not need to make changes in their physician–patient, their banking, or their congregational membership relations. Often their move is only for a short distance. Where such changes are needed, the majority make them within the first three months of their new residency.

The next tier of relationships, in which about 60% experienced changes, includes: registering to vote, making a nonwork acquaintance, and making at least one close friend. Here again the majority make these changes within the first three months.

The two areas in which adjustments extend over more than three months for at least 25 percent of the persons are in registering to vote and in feeling "at home" in the new location.

At least 25% in the South and West also require more than three months to make a close friendship in their new location.

For clergy the impact of residential/occupational mobility is much greater than for laity. They are more likely to move for work-related reasons and to move longer distances. Therefore, in from 80 to 90 percent of all cases they must make changes in their institutional and personal relationships.

The changes made most quickly by clergy, in three months or less by about 80 percent, are in their banking affiliation, congregation membership, and making nonwork acquaintances. A majority, ranging from 61 percent to 52 percent, register to vote, relate to a new physician, and make one close friendship, within three months of the move. The adjustment that takes the longest is feeling at home. For nearly one-half (48%) this takes longer than three months, for 14 percent more than one year. Institutional adjustments come more quickly than do psychological adjustments.

Postscript

Considering where they live—regionally and size of community—Lutherans are not in the power centers of the nation. Regionally and locally they may indeed have considerable influence. Nationally they are out of the mainstream.

Why is it that though the nation's population balance shifted south and west during the 1970s the Lutheran regional membership distribution remained unchanged?

Lutheran young people aged 21-27—as their age group generally—make at least several moves in the process of establishing themselves in their adult roles. Yet the adjustment they most often feel is not needed is that of changing their congregation membership. Four out of five must learn to feel at home in the new location, two out of three must make new acquaintances and friends, half must change their banking affiliations. Only one in four needs to change congregation membership. Why the difference? Is congregation membership unimportant? Is the home congregation membership a symbol of security and stability amidst changes? Does the home congregation hang on unduly, doing nothing to assist the person to transfer membership to a new congregation?

Clergy know firsthand the types of adjustments mobility requires of young adults. They could help the congregation, and its members, to increased sensitivity and increased effectiveness in work with mobile, seeking, searching, ofttimes uncertain young adults.

8

Who Are the Lutherans?

Now that we know so much else about Lutherans, it's time to identify them as human beings. Among them are more women than men. There are more middle-aged persons and fewer young children and fewer elderly persons, as well as a larger percent of married persons among Lutherans than in the general population. They're largely of German and Scandinavian ancestry, educated beyond the high school level, and are employed, most often in white-collar occupations.

Gender and Age

Women outnumber men among the lay respondents by a 57 to 43 percent margin. Put another way, there are only 77 male respondents for every 100 female respondents. The disparity is greatest in the 21-35 age range, where less than 65 men respond for every 100 women. The disparity is least in the over 65 age bracket. (See Table 18.)

The 4371 lay respondents live in households with a total membership of 12,856 persons. In this total household membership an unusual situation prevails. Where both age and gender

92 Who Are the Lutherans?

Table 18. Age Group Distribution and Gender Ratios, Respondents and All Household Members, and Gender Ratio for U.S. White Population, 1979 for Selected Age Groups

Age Group	% of Each Age Group Total in Specific Age Group		Number of Males per 100 Females by Age Groups		
	Respondents	House-hold Members	Respondents	House-hold Members	U.S. Population
0- 4	0	5.4	—	100 ⎞	
5- 9	0	6.6	—	96 ⎬	105
10-15	1.5	11.1	75	94 ⎠	
16-20	6.9	11.6	69	97 ⎞	102
21-25	5.3	5.7	56	90 ⎠	
26-35	19.8	12.9	64	85 ⎞	99
36-45	17.5	13.6	83	95 ⎠	
46-55	17.8	13.4	74	89 ⎞	93
56-65	17.9	11.7	88	114 ⎠	
Over 65	13.3	8.0	95	107	68
Total, all laity for whom age and gender are known	100.0	100.0	77	96	95

are known, there are more men than women aged 56 and older and fewer boys than girls in ages 5-20. Both of these factors are quite unlike population data generally. Lutherans appear to have fewer males, proportionately in ages under 45 and more in ages over 45 than is true for the nation's population as a whole. Yet, among both Lutheran households and among the nation's population there are about 95 men for every 100 women.

Roughly one-third of the lay respondents fall into one or the other of three major age groups. Those under 36 years of age account for 34 percent of all respondents, those between 36 and 55 for 35 percent, and those over 55 for 31 percent.

The members of the respondent households also fall about evenly into three major, but different, age groups. Roughly one-third are under 21 (35%), one-third are between 21 and 45 (32%) and one-third are over 45 (33%).

Almost universally, the clergy are male. Three of every five are 45 or younger. Their families, unlike those of the laity, include more male than female members by a 52 to 48 percent margin. Their families also are younger than those of the laity respondents. One-third (31%) of their household members are 15 or younger, another one-third (31%) are 16 to 35 years of age. Only 21 percent are older than 45.

Noteworthy too is the fact that the clergy households are larger than those of the laity households. Whereas laity households average 2.88 members, clergy households average 3.80 members. This one-member difference no doubt stems largely from the younger age of the clergy families. Fewer members as yet have left the family nest.

For comparison, the average household size in the U.S.A. in 1980 was 2.75 members. It would appear that Lutheran laity are fairly close to the American average in household size, clergy significantly larger.

Data for the total membership of Lutheran laity households indicate the median age to be around 33. For the nation as a whole the median age is around 29. Thus, members of the Lutheran households included in this survey are older than the national average.

Yet here, too, an unusual difference appears. Lutheran households, compared with the nation's population, include markedly fewer children under five years of age and markedly fewer persons over the age of 65. Conversely, these households include markedly more persons in the 45-64 age range. These differences appear not only in the overall total, but also in each of the four regions of the U.S.A. (See Table 19.)

Family Status

Three-fourths of the respondents are currently married, more likely among men (84%) than among women (70%). Only

Table 19. Age Group Comparison, Profiles Total Laity Household Membership with U.S. Population, 1979 by Regions

Population Group and Region	Percent of Population in Age Group				
	Under 5 years	5-24 years	25-44 years	45-64 years	Over 64
Total Profiles households	5.4	35.0	26.5	25.1	8.0
Total U.S.	7.1	34.5	27.2	19.9	11.3
Northeast, Profiles	5.1	35.9	28.6	22.6	7.8
Northeast, U.S.	6.1	33.2	26.9	21.7	12.1
North Central, Profiles	5.6	35.8	25.5	25.0	8.1
North Central, U.S.	7.1	35.1	27.0	19.6	11.2
South, Profiles	4.9	31.5	26.9	27.8	8.9
South, U.S.	7.4	34.9	27.1	19.3	11.3
West, Profiles	5.7	33.5	27.2	27.2	6.4
West, U.S.	7.8	34.5	28.2	19.5	10.0

one in 100 men but ten in 100 women is widowed. The highest ratios of married persons are found among the clergy and among laity aged 45-55. In each instance 90 percent are married. Being widowed, of course, is a significant reality for the over 55 group, where 17 percent have lost their spouse to death.

Lutheran households include a much larger proportion of married persons than is true for the nation as a whole. Considering only persons 18 years of age and older, 77 percent of the adult Lutherans, compared with 66 percent of the nation's adults, are married. Proportionately, only half as many Lutherans are widowed, divorced, or separated as among the nation's people. Somewhat fewer Lutherans (16%) have never been married, compared with 20 percent for the nation's people.

Though the term may not be in current favor, nine of every ten men, one of every four women, respondents is recognized as "head of the household." Several two-thirds patterns appear among the respondents. Two-thirds (68%) of those under 21 are children of the head of the household; two-thirds (65%) of the women are his spouse; two-thirds (68%) of those over 55 are head of the household. Respondents between the ages of 21 and 55 are fairly evenly divided between spouse and head.

Considering all members of the household, 57 percent of the males, nine percent of the women, are accepted as head. Nearly 40 percent of both the male and the female members are children of the one who heads the family. Parents and siblings of the respondents make up one percent each of the male, two percent each of the female, members of these households.

Ancestral Background—Respondent

The lineage of Lutherans is overwhelmingly German and Scandinavian. A strong majority (around 58%) of Lutherans—both men and women, of all age groups, and in every geographic region except the West—is of German ancestry. Even in the West, German ancestry persons comprise a majority (51%) of the Lutherans in that region.

Scandinavian ancestry Lutherans are most prominent in the North Central and West. Here they account for 27 or 28 percent of the Lutheran membership. In contrast, Scandinavian ancestry persons account for only seven percent of the Lutherans in the South and 11 percent in the Northeast.

Lutheran youth (under 21 years of age) stem somewhat more often from German and somewhat less often from Scandinavian lineage than do Lutherans over 55 years of age. The comparable ratios for the under 21 group are 61 percent German, 16 percent Scandinavian. For the older age group the comparable ratios are 57 percent German, 24 percent Scandinavian.

The third largest ancestral group for Lutherans totally is English—11 percent. In the South, however, persons of English lineage are the second largest group—21 percent of the Lutheran membership. In the Northeast persons of English, Scandinavian, and European ancestry other than German are equally included in the Lutheran membership.

Lutheran clergy are more overwhelmingly German (65%) and Scandinavian (24%) in ancestry than are the laity. The remaining 11 percent are about evenly divided between other European and English ancestries.

Ancestral Background—Spouse

When Lutherans marry, they usually marry a person who also is of either German or Scandinavian ancestry. A clear majority (around 55%) of both men and women marry a person of German ancestry. Exceptions to this majority pattern occur only among the few youth (under 21) who are married and among Lutherans in the West. Even in these exceptional instances, however, 42 percent of the youth and 47 percent of the Lutherans in the West are married to a spouse of German ancestry.

Scandinavian ancestry spouses are second most numerous (1) for both men and women, (2) among persons over 35 years of age, and (3) among married couples in the North Central and West. In each instance they comprise between 16 and 24 percent of the spouses.

The exceptions to the Scandinavian plurality perhaps are significant. One, almost half of the married youth (under 21) give no ancestral information on their spouse. Two, more of the young adults (21-35 years of age) marry persons of "other European" than of Scandinavian ancestry. Three, Lutherans in the South are four times as likely to have a spouse of English ancestry (20%) as one of Scandinavian ancestry (5%). Four, in the Northeast, spouses of English and of other European ancestry equal 13 or 14 percent of all spouses, compared with seven percent who are of Scandinavian lineage.

Again, clergy more consistently than laity marry spouses from the dominant German and Scandinavian ancestry lines. Some 59 percent are of German, 25 percent of Scandinavian lineage. Ten percent of the clergy spouses are of English ancestry.

Educational Levels

The majority of Lutherans have a formal education that includes at least some college or technical-school experience. Indeed, some 30 percent of the men, and nearly 20 percent of the women, whether respondents or spouses, have completed at least a baccalaureate degree. (See Table 20.)

Table 20. Educational Level of Respondents and Spouses

Group	Percent of Each Group Completing Formal Education at Level Indicated				
	Less than high school graduation	*High school graduate*	*Some college or technical*	*Baccalaureate degree*	*Postgraduate study*
Lay respondents, total	16	28	33	11	12
Male respondents	17	23	30	14	16
Female respondents	13	33	35	10	9
Spouses of respondents					
Wives	10	38	33	11	8
Husbands	16	27	29	14	14
Clergy respondents	0	1	2	5	92
Clergy spouses	1	11	39	27	22
Respondents, aged 36-55	6	33	33	13	15
Respondents, aged over 55	25	30	30	6	8

Lutheran clergy, of course, almost universally have a formal educational level beyond the baccalaureate degree. Their spouses, too, have a notably higher educational level than have the laity. Virtually half (49%) have completed at least a college degree. The data suggest that among Lutherans higher education is an opportunity more likely to be available for men than for women.

A major difference appears in the educational levels of those respondents over 55 compared with those aged 36-55. (Refer again to Table 20.) One-fourth of the respondents over 55 years of age stopped their formal schooling short of high school graduation. In contrast, more than one-fourth of those between the ages of 36 and 55 have at least a baccalaureate degree.

A regional difference not shown in tabular form is the higher educational level of Lutherans in the South and West compared with those in the North Central states. This fact is true for both respondents and spouses. Around 30 percent in the South and West, around 20 percent in North Central, have completed at least a baccalaureate degree.

Employment Status

Most Lutheran men respondents are employed, either full time (57%), or part time (5%). Some 15 percent are self-employed. About one in five (19%) is retired. Involuntary unemployment is rare, idling only two percent.

Lutheran women respondents are homemakers (37%), are employed full time (29%) or part time (22%), or regard themselves as retired (13%).

Spouses of the respondents show similar employment patterns. Husbands of the women respondents are somewhat more likely to be employed full time, somewhat less likely to be retired, than are the men respondents. Wives of the respondents are a bit more likely to be homemakers, a bit less likely to be employed, than are the women respondents themselves.

Half of the clergy spouses are homemakers. The majority of the clergy spouses are employed outside the home, 21 percent on a full-time, 33 percent on a part-time basis.

As would be expected, the majority of youth (under 21) attend school, though more than 40 percent also hold jobs. Again as expected, a 70 percent majority of those aged 21-55 are employed. Nearly half (47%) of those in the over 55 age group regard themselves as retired.

The only notable regional variation is the relatively high proportion (11%) of self-employed persons in the North Central states. In the Northeast the comparable proportion is four percent.

Occupation Categories

Nearly 60 percent of Lutheran men are likely to be professionals, proprietors (including farm operators), or craftsmen. Nearly 70 percent of Lutheran women are either homemakers, clerical workers, or professional persons.

Occupationally grouped another way, half of Lutheran men are employed in white-collar, one-fourth in blue-collar jobs. One-fifth are either retired or students. The remaining five percent are in such service positions as police and fire protection, armed services, and barbers. Similarly grouped occupationally, about 45 percent of Lutheran women are homemakers, students, or retired persons. About 45 percent are employed in white-collar occupations. The remaining 10 percent are about equally divided between the blue-collar and the service occupations.

Detailed data appear in Table 21, covering respondents and spouses.

Regional variations are minimal, with one exception. Both respondents and spouses in the South and the West are more likely to be professional persons than are their fellow Lutherans in the Northeast or the North Central.

Several age factors stand out. Professional persons are particularly numerous in the ages between 21 and 55. Proprietors, managers, and officials are more numerous in the 36-55 age group than in any other. In giving their occupational status, nearly 30 percent of both respondents and spouses over the age of 55 call themselves retired. The 17 percentage points difference between this figure and that given under employment status is understandable. Retired persons often regard themselves occupationally in accord with the kind of work they did prior to their retirement.

Table 21. Percent of Laity Respondents and Spouses
by Occupation Category

Occupation Category	Males		Females	
	Respondents	Husbands	Respondents	Wives
White collar				
Professional, technical, kindred	25	23	17	18
Proprietors, managers, officials	16	15	3	5
Sales workers	6	8	2	3
Clerical and related	4	4	22	15
Blue collar				
Craftsmen, foremen, and related	16	20	2	1
Operatives and related	2	3	2	2
Laborers	6	7	1	1
Service workers	5	3	4	5
Homemakers	1	1	28	36
Students	7	°	8	°
Retired	12	9	8	10
Not answered	°	7	3	4

° Less than 0.05 percent

Postscript

This survey reinforces the picture of U.S. Lutherans as family people of Northern European ancestry, employed in positions on the upper-middle rungs on the occupational ladder. What is surprising is the comparative absence of young children and the elderly. Perhaps it is a peculiarity of the sample. Or, perhaps it tells us that Lutheran congregations appeal particularly to husband-and-wife couples, within the age of 35 and 65, together with their children still living at home.

Reaching out to and bringing the unchurched into Lutheran

church membership seems not to be a Lutheran strength. If the unchurched include sizable numbers of persons who are of Asiatic, Black, Hispanic, Indian, or South European ancestry, what would make them feel comfortable in a congregation whose members are primarily of Northern European ancestry? If the unchurched include sizable numbers of single persons, young adults without children, divorced persons rearing children as single parents, and the elderly who have lost their ties with family, what would make them feel comfortable in a congregation whose members primarily cluster in "normal" families?

Are Lutheran congregations truly ready to reach out to and genuinely to welcome into their circles people who are "different" from the present members? Do Lutheran congregations implicitly limit God's love for the world (John 3:16) to the Northern European segment thereof? Do Lutheran congregations demonstrate that the one thing needful (Luke 10:42) is for not only the Marys and Marthas but also for today's equivalents of the publicans and sinners found in every community?

Of all human needs, is not the greatest the need to hear the good news of life and salvation through Jesus Christ?

Appendix A
Methods Used in the Study

In celebration of the 450th anniversary of the Augsburg Confession and Luther's Small Catechism, and the 400th anniversary of the Book of Concord, Aid Association for Lutherans (AAL), Appleton, Wisconsin, sponsored a study of members of Lutheran churches in the United States.

The general aims and specific objectives of the study were established in 1979 by a steering committee, consisting of representatives from eight participating Lutheran church bodies and from the Lutheran Council in the U.S.A. The general purpose of the study was to gather information useful for understanding Lutheran membership, facilitating future planning, and supplying specific information to church bodies. These aims were to be accomplished by collecting data from Lutheran laity, clergy, and, in some church bodies, teachers, on such matters as: demographics; family information; mobility; financial status; reasons for and experiences in being Lutheran; attitudes about the church, the role of women, and other social issues; worship and other religious activities and experiences; and financial contributions.

Through a consensus process a common core of question

areas of interest to all eight church bodies was identified by the steering committee. A draft survey instrument was prepared, containing these core items, along with sets of other questions unique to the different church bodies. Under the leadership of Dr. Alan C. Klass, director of Corporate Research at Aid Association for Lutherans, the data collection methods, including the sampling and data analysis plans, also were devised and approved by the steering committee.

In June 1980 AAL contracted with National Family Opinion, Inc. (NFO) to carry out the data collection, the codification and initial analyses of the data, and to prepare a series of tabulations and narrative reports for the steering committee that summarized the findings for each church body and for the Lutheran population as a whole. The latter were weighted proportionately to reflect the membership strength of each church body.

The method of data collection was a self-administered mail questionnaire. The number of questions in the instrument varied somewhat for the different church bodies, but some 81 items constitute the common "core" discussed in this volume. Depending on the church body involved, the mail questionnaire was a printed booklet of 16 to 20 pages, legal size.

The selection of lay member and clergy respondents for the sample took place through a series of stages. A systematic sampling procedure was used, with the aim of identifying about 1570 clergy, 600 teachers, and 18,000 lay members, selected from geographic areas corresponding to U.S. Census regions. Because the parish was the point of contact to identify respondents, parish size was stratified. Unlike some other projects which seek responses from many members in a few congregations, this one sought responses from one or a few members in each of many congregations.

An initial contact letter was sent to the parish pastor, explaining the purpose of the study and the steps the pastor should follow in selecting potential lay respondents, employing a random procedure in selecting representative lay members from the parish. The pastor also provided some background information on each of the persons selected to be invited to participate.

After National Family Opinion had received the names of potential respondents, its staff sent the survey instruments either directly to the congregation members named by the pastors or to the participating church bodies for their subsequent distribution to their potential respondents. Two reminder letters and questionnaires were sent to those persons who did not respond to the initial mailing. The cut-off date for processing of returns was January 31, 1981.

Three separate investigations (using clergy-supplied information about persons they nominated, making follow-up telephone calls to some 400 nonrespondents, and examining response patterns from reminder mailings) were carried out to determine possible biases in the total responses received. Virtually no bias was detected on age, sex, mobility, education, income, occupation, optimism/pessimism, "born again," and most other items. Some minor bias was discovered, however, in that respondents tended somewhat more than nonrespondents to attend church regularly and to contribute more generously.

The data analysis and reporting took the form of preparing summary tables for each item, showing the percentage of respondents giving each response option. These percentages were reported separately for teachers, clergy, and for total lay members, and for lay members differentiated according to sex, six age categories, and four geographic regions. (Data for teachers are not reported in this volume since they are members primarily of two church bodies.)

Just over one-half of the congregations, of the laity, and of the clergy contacted provided data requested for this project. The number of responses received prior to the January 31, 1981, deadline date and used as the basis of this report, with major breakdowns, is:

Churches Contacted	5,412	
Churches Agreeing to Participate	2,885	53%
Lay People Contacted	7,888	
Total Lay Members Participating	4,371	55%

Gender
Male	1,721
Female	2,295
No answer	35

Age
Under 21	309
21-27	309
28-35	610
36-44	585
45-55	705
56 and over	1,143
No answer	390

Region
North East	743
North Central	2,584
South	576
West	468

Total Nonidentifiable by Age or Sex	320	
Clergy Contacted	1,570	
Total Clergy Participating	886	56%
Teachers Contacted	500	
Total Teachers Participating	377	75%

In reporting findings, subgroup differences, e.g., between males and females, are generally not reported unless they differed by at least five percentage points from the average for the total laity. Thus, if differences are not noted, it can be assumed that the differences, if any, are relatively minor and thus of no probable importance.

Appendix B
Profiles of Lutherans Questionnaire

Appendix B provides as information the text of the instructions and of the core questions which were used by all participating church bodies. These core questions comprise about 75 percent of all questions used. Each church body added further questions of particular interest to that church body.

The text as here presented is condensed so as to eliminate excess pages. A copy of the full questionnaire can be obtained by writing the appropriate person listed in Appendix C.

Invitation to Participation

Thank you for your participation. We are grateful for your contribution of time and effort. The results will help us to better understand our membership, facilitate future planning, and supply specific information helpful in program structure. These decisions can be better made if we know about Lutherans' characteristics and attitudes on more than "church things." Some of the questions may surprise you. They are asked because the information is needed, not out of simple curiosity.

Who should complete this questionnaire: This questionnaire should be completed only by the person whose name appears on the envelope in which it came. If necessary, please forward this questionnaire to that person. If the addressee is unable to complete the questionnaire, please write the reason here, and return this questionnaire using the accompanying return envelope.

General instructions:

1. Mark your answers directly on this questionnaire in the spaces provided, using either pencil or pen.
2. The ways for indicating your answers to the questions vary:
   — Some questions have lines beside the possible answers. Indicate your answer by writing an X on the appropriate line.
     Example: Sex. __ Male __ Female
   — Some questions have numbers to be circled to show your opinion or thinking.
     Example: Generally speaking, what are your feelings about the coming 10 years with respect to: Country
              Pessimistic   −2 −1 0 +1 +2   Optimistic
     In this example, if you are pessimistic about your country's next 10 years you would circle −2. If you are optimistic, you would circle 2. If you are somewhere between pessimistic and optimistic, you would indicate where between circling either −1, 0, or 1.
   — Some questions have a line for you to write a number in.
     Example: How many years have you lived in your current residence? _____ years
3. Unless otherwise instructed, mark (X, circle, or write in) one answer per question.
4. **WORK ALONE** except for those few questions where you need facts from another family member. The method of picking people to participate in the survey makes it *important* that only *your* attitudes, opinions or judgements are recorded on the survey.

Do not worry about the fact that the questions are not numbered in sequence. The questions have been numbered so as to reduce the cost of entering information into a computer for analysis.

A note about certain terms: Throughout this questionnaire, the term *"congregation"* is used to refer to the congregation in which you are a member. The term *"your pastor"* is used to refer generally to the pastor or pastors of your congregation.

When you have completed this questionnaire, please return it using the accompanying postage paid return envelope.

PROFILES OF LUTHERANS
Core Questions

DESCRIBE YOURSELF
(and your spouse if you are now married)

The church could be more helpful to the many different people who are Lutheran if more were known about who they are. Please describe yourself (and your spouse if you are *now married)* using the questions in this section. If you are not now married, mark here _____ and skip the "spouse" column in each question.

1. What is your and your spouse's *predominant* ancestral background? MARK ONE PER COLUMN. *0. Not now married 1. German 2. Scandinavian 3. English 4. Other European (e.g., French, Italian) 5. African 6. Spanish/Hispanic 7. Asian (Far Eastern) 8. Near/Middle Eastern 9. American Indian 10. Other*

2. In what denomination were you (and your spouse) raised? MARK ONE PER COLUMN *0. Not now married 1. Lutheran 2. Baptist 3. Methodist 4. Presbyterian 5. Pentecostal 6. Episcopal 7. Roman Catholic 8. None 9. Do not know 10. Other*

3. Between your original denomination and now, were you (and your spouse) ever a member of another denomination(s)? _____ No. Skip to question 4 _____ Yes. Which one? MARK ALL THAT APPLY. *0. Not now married 1. Lutheran 2. Baptist 3. Methodist 4. Presbyterian 5. Pentecostal 6. Episcopal 7. Roman Catholic 8. None 9. Do not know 10. Other*

5. What is your (and your spouse's) employment status MARK ALL THAT APPLY *0. Not now married 1. Employed full time 2. Employed part time 3. Self employed 4. Homemaker 5. Not employed but able to work 6. Unable to work 7. Going to school 8. Retired 9. Other*

6. What is your (and your spouse's) *PRIMARY* occupation category? MARK ONE PER COLUMN *0. Not now married 1. Armed forces 2. Clerical and related workers 3. Craftsmen, foremen and related workers 4. Homemakers 5. Laborers 6. Operatives and related workers 7. Private household workers 8. Professional, technical and similar workers 9. Proprietors, managers and officials 10. Sales workers 11. Service workers, except private household workers 12. Students 13. Retired persons 14. Other*

8. What is your (and your spouse's) highest education level? MARK ONE PER COLUMN *0. Not now married   1. 8th grade or less   2. 9th-11th grade   3. 12th grade (or equivalency test)   4. Some college but no college degree or diploma   5. Completed technical or trade program   6. Associate degree   7. Bachelor's degree   8. Some graduate work   9. Advanced degree*

ACTIVITIES

The next group of questions has to do with the types of activities in which people participate *other than* employment, homemaking, sleeping, eating, or commuting to work.

13. *Approximately* what percent of a typical week do you spend in each of the following groups of activities? Total to 100%

    _____% *Home care*   _____% *Income production*
    _____% *Volunteer*   _____% *Personal activities*
    _____% *In transit*

14. Below are listed several types of groups or organizations. Please indicate *how many* of each type you are affiliated with. MARK ALL WITH "0", "1", "2" ETC. *1. Service club   2. Veterans group   3. Political group   4. Social-action group   5. Fraternal group   6. Labor union   7. Sports group   8. Senior-citizen group   9. Literary, discussion, study group   10. Self-improvement group   11. Personal-support group   12. Youth group   13. School service group   14. Hobby club   15. Ethnic organization   16. Church-affiliated group   17. Farm organization   18. Performing-arts group   19. Professional organization   20. Other (specify)*

If you are not affiliated with any groups or organizations, mark here _____ and skip to question 29.

15. Decide which group or organization on which you spend the MOST time. What type of group or organization, as listed in question 14 above, is it? *Number _____ (from the list in question 14)*

16. In what manner do you participate in that organization? MARK ONE *1. Leader   2. Active worker   3. Regular participant   4. Occasional participant*

17. What is the strongest reason why you participate? MARK ONE *1. Feel an obligation   2. Family member(s) or friend(s) participate   3. Satisfaction/my volunteer service is needed   4. Enjoyment/fun   5. A way to support the cause   6. Other*

18. How much personal satisfaction do you get from participation?
    CIRCLE ONE NUMBER   *None*   *1   2   3   4   5*
    A great deal
19. How much personal interest do you have in the group?   *None*
    1   2   3   4   5   A great deal
20. Decide which group or organization on which you spend the
    SECOND MOST time. What type of group organization, as
    listed in question 14 above, is it? The second group may be of
    the *same type* as the first group which you used for the "most
    time".   *Number _____ (the list in question 14)*
21. In what manner do you participate? MARK ONE   *1. Leader
    2. Active worker   3. Regular participant   4. Occasional par-
    ticipant*
22. What is the strongest reason why you participate? MARK ONE
    *1. Feel an obligation   2. Family member(s) or friend(s) par-
    ticipate   3. Satisfaction/my volunteer service is needed   4. En-
    joyment/fun   5. A way to support the cause   6. Other*
23. How much personal satisfaction do you get from participation?
    None   1   2   3   4   5   A great deal
24. How much personal interest do you have in the group?
    None   1   2   3   4   5   A great deal
29. Some people get involved in local, state or national causes such
    as hospital auxiliary, rights protection, divorce law changes,
    gun control, etc. In *Column A* please list those causes which
    you are concerned about. In *Column B* please mark whether
    or not you are active.
    *[Three lines each provided to list local, state, and national
    causes.]*

WORSHIP EXPERIENCE

The following questions will help us better understand how members feel about worship.

30. When asked why they attend church, people say that they at-
    tend for several reasons. Usually people have more than one
    reason. Very often people answer with the "stock" or "correct"
    answer even if it is not their strongest reason for attending.
    From the list below please *mark one* choice which is your *most
    strongly* felt reason for attending church worship when you
    attend. Please *mark only one*, even though you may have sev-
    eral. MARK ONE   *1. Someone requires that I attend   2. I
    feel a general sense of obligation to attend   3. I enjoy being
    with the people (sense of community)   4. I enjoy participating*

in the service/hearing the pastor   5. To experience the feeling of praising God   6. Need to hear God's word   7. To worship God   8. To feel God's presence   9. Other

32. On Sunday mornings, most congregations use predominantly one or two orders of worship (liturgy). At your church, how frequently have you experienced an order of worship other than your congregation's regular orders of worship within the past year?   *About _____ times.*

33. Generally speaking, how satisfying have you found worship services in your congregation when a different order of worship is used?

    Not satisfying   1   2   3   4   5   Very satisfying
    Not worshipful   1   2   3   4   5   Very worshipful

43. Below are listed several types of worship experiences. Indicate the frequency of these experiences in your life during the PAST YEAR: MARK SOMETHING FOR EACH LINE   *Attend Sunday worship services, Sunday School or Bible Class, Receive communion, Personal/private devotions, Home family devotions, Bible reading, Listening to religious radio, Watching religious television, Attend other religious gathering, Say grace at mealtime, Pray privately, Other*
    [Frequency options listed were: none, 1-5 times, 6-12 times, 13-36 times, weekly, daily.]

BEING LUTHERAN

The next group of questions will help us understand what being a Lutheran means to you. It will also help us to know how members of our church feel about the other Lutheran groups.

44. How did you come to be a Lutheran? MARK ONE   *1. Reared as Lutheran   2. Marriage-related situation   3. Through an acquaintance   4. I sought a church and chose Lutheran   5. Helped through a life trauma/crisis by a Lutheran   6. Visited by or liked the pastor   7. Attracted by programs or educational opportunities   8. Availability of Christian day school   9. Other*

51. If you had to move to an area which did not have another (church body name) congregation, but did have another Lutheran congregation, generally how upsetting would that be to you?   CIRCLE ONE NUMBER
    Not upsetting   1   2   3   4   5   Very upsetting

52. If you had to move to an area which did not have another Lu-

theran congregation of any kind, generally how upsetting would that be to you? CIRCLE ONE NUMBER

Not upsetting   *1*   *2*   *3*   *4*   *5*   *Very upsetting*

55. There are several different Lutheran church bodies. Generally how different do you feel these Lutheran church bodies are from each other? MARK ONE   *1. I do not know. Skip to question 61*   *2. Really not different. Skip to question 61*   *3. Slightly different*   *4. Moderately different*   *5. Quite different*   *6. Extremely different*

56. What percentages would you assign to the reasons listed below for these differences? ____*% Doctrinal* ____*% Political/Organizational* ____*% Historical/Ancestral*

61. Would you say that you have been "born again" or have had a "born again" experience—that is, a turning point in your life when you committed yourself to Christ?   *1. Yes*   *2. No*

62. Have you ever had a religious experience—that is a particularly powerful religious insight or awakening that changed the direction of your life?   *1. Yes*   *2. No*   *3. Don't know*

63. Would you consider yourself a Pentecostal or Charismatic Christian?   *1. Yes*   *2. No*   *3. Don't know*

64. How important to you are your religious beliefs?   *1. Very important*   *2. Fairly important*   *3. Not too important*   *4. Not at all important*   *5. No opinion*

65. At the present time, do you think religion as a whole is increasing its influence on American life or losing its influence?   *1. Increasing*   *2. Losing*   *3. Same*   *4. Don't know*

The next seven questions deal with some (not all) Lutheran beliefs. The questions will help us compare what Lutherans thought in 1970 with what Lutherans think in 1980. These questions do not cover all aspects of Lutheran belief.

71. The account of Adam and Eve falling into sinfulness is simply a story which did NOT take place in reality.   *1. Agree*   *2. Probably agree*   *3. Not sure*   *4. Probably disagree*   *5. Disagree*   *6. No opinion*

72. Only those who believe in Jesus Christ as their Savior can go to heaven.   *1. Agree*   *2. Probably agree*   *3. Not sure*   *4. Probably disagree*   *5. Disagree*   *6. No opinion*

73. A child is already sinful at birth.   *1. Agree*   *2. Probably agree*   *3. Not sure*   *4. Probably disagree*   *5. Disagree*   *6. No opinion*

74. The main emphasis of the Gospel is on God's rules for right living.   *1. Agree*   *2. Probably agree*   *3. Not sure*   *4. Probably disagree*   *5. Disagree*   *6. No opinion*

75. Although there are many religions in the world, most of them

lead to the same God. *1. Agree   2. Probably agree   3. Not sure   4. Probably disagree   5. Disagree   6. No opinion*

76. God is satisfied if a person lives the best life one can. *1. Agree   2. Probably agree   3. Not sure   4. Probably disagree   5. Disagree   6. No opinion*

77. Property (house, automobile, money, investments, etc.) belongs to God; we only hold it in trust for God. *1. Agree   2. Probably agree   3. Not sure   4. Probably disagree   5. Disagree   6. No opinion*

79. Do you receive information about the activities of the (church body name)? *1. No. Skip to question 80   2. Yes.* Which of the following are the *primary* sources of your information about _____ activities? MARK ALL THAT APPLY *3. Pastor   4. Congregation's bulletin or newsletter   5. Church publication   6. The local newspaper   7. Other*

80. Listed below are religious television or radio programs. Mark how frequently you watch or listen to EACH. If you watch or listen to others, please list them also. *Billy Graham   Oral Roberts   This Is the Life   P.T.L.   The Lutheran Hour   Robert Schuller   Rex Humbard   Other*

[*Frequency options listed were: almost every week, once or twice a month, several times a year, rarely, never.*]

81. About how much money did you contribute last year either *directly* or by receiving a return gift acknowledging a contribution to the production of   *Lutheran television/radio programming,   Other religious television/radio programming*
$_____ $_____

ROLE AND FUTURE OF THE CHURCH

Although [church body name] is not meant to be run by public opinion poll, the administrators are interested in knowing what members feel about the role and future of the church.

84. Below are listed several choices which could be described as "the purpose of a local congregation." Place a "1" by the choice which you feel is the most important function of a *local congregation.* Place a "2" for the second, and "3" for the third most important function and so on until you have ranked *what you feel* are the TOP 6 functions for the local congregation.
    Sunday morning worship,   Holy Communion,   Bible study for adults,   Fellowship occasions (i.e., dinners, picnics),   Service projects to meet local social concerns,

Christian education of children,   Church sponsored rec-reational activities,   Members' support for one another in time of need,   Weekday prayer or worship services,   Small groups for sharing personal insights or concerns,   Youth programs,   Ministry of service to persons with special needs,   Opportunities to participate in the broader work of the church,   Bring new members into the church,   Evangelism

92. In what manner do you feel that the church should be involved in the issues listed below: MARK AS MANY AS APPLY TO EACH

    MARK   *IF YOU FEEL THAT:*
    None   the church should not be involved at all
    Memb.   church members as individuals should be involved
    Serm.   discussion of this issue is appropriate in sermons
    Cong.   local congregations as congregations should be in-volved

    XXXX   the XXXX as a church body should officially become involved

    Rights of minorities
    Church-government relationships
    Local zoning laws
    Handling of crime and criminals
    Equal treatment under the law
    Substance abuse prevention
    Medical care issues
    Elections and candidates
    Business-government relationships
    Education in public schools

103. Generally speaking, what are your feelings about the coming 10 years with respect to: CIRCLE ONE NUMBER ON EACH LINE

    Pessimistic -2 -1 0 $+1$ $+2$ Optimistic

Country	-2	-1	0	$+1$	$+2$
World affairs	-2	-1	0	$+1$	$+2$
(Church body)	-2	-1	0	$+1$	$+2$
Local congregation	-2	-1	0	$+1$	$+2$
National economy	-2	-1	0	$+1$	$+2$
Personal finances	-2	-1	0	$+1$	$+2$
Your personal future	-2	-1	0	$+1$	$+2$
Your family relations	-2	-1	0	$+1$	$+2$

ROLES OF WOMEN

Discussions on roles of women are frequently heard in society today. We are interested in your opinion on the following eight questions concerning roles of women.

113. It is somehow unnatural to place women in positions of authority over men.
    Strongly Disagree   –2   –1   0   +1   +2   *Strongly Agree*

114. It is more unfair for a woman to desert her family than for a man to do so.
    Strongly Disagree   –2   –1   0   +1   +2   *Strongly Agree*

115. Some equality in the marriage is a good thing, but by and large the husband should have the final word in family matters.
    Strongly Disagree   –2   –1   0   +1   +2   *Strongly Agree*

116. Women rely more on intuition and less on reason than men do.
    Strongly Disagree   –2   –1   0   +1   +2   *Strongly Agree*

117. A mother should have primary responsibility for the care and nurture of children.
    Strongly Disagree   –2   –1   0   +1   +2   *Strongly Agree*

118. A married woman with small children has as much right as her husband to work outside the home.
    Strongly Disagree   –2   –1   0   +1   +2   *Strongly Agree*

119. Raising children is the most important thing a woman can do.
    Strongly Disagree   –2   –1   0   +1   +2   *Strongly Agree*

120. Compared with men, women should receive equal pay for equal work.
    Strongly Disagree   –2   –1   0   +1   +2   *Strongly Agree*

RESIDENCE AND MOBILITY

The next section will help us learn about the characteristics of and reasons why people live where they live and move from place to place.

131. What is your zip code? __ __ __ __ __

132. Which of these categories comes closest to the type of place where you live? MARK ONE   *1. metropolis over 1,000,000*
    2. suburb of a metropolis   3. large city (250,000 to 1,000,000)
    4. suburb of a large city   5. medium city (50,000 to 250,000)
    6. suburb of a medium city   7. small city (10,000 to 50,000)
    8. town of 2,500 to 10,000   9. rural town (under 2,500)
    10. rural or farm (open country)

133. In which state is your *current* residence located? _____

134. How many years have you lived in your current residence (dwelling)? _____

135. How many miles are there between your current residence (dwelling) and your most recent former residence (dwelling)? _____ *miles* _____ *Never moved*   SKIP TO QUESTION 140

136. In which state was your *most recent* former residence located?

_____

137. Which of the statements below best describe the *reason for* your most recent move? MARK ONE   *1. change in quality of life (climate, atmosphere, etc.)   2. changing neighborhood   3. health related reason   4. job related reason   5. family related reason (including marriage)   6. other*

138. Which of the changes listed below occurred with your *most recent* change of residence? MARK ALL THAT APPLY *1. Change in size of community   2. Change in size of dwelling   3. Change from owner-to-renter or renter-to-owner   4. Proximity to religious facility (church, school, etc.)   5. Proximity to other facility (job, education, factory)   6. Proximity to family or friend   7. Job change, transfer, or retirement   8. Change of health or comfort   9. Other*

139. Are you living in the same residence as you were 5 YEARS AGO? *1. Yes   Skip to question 140   2. No   If no, which of these categories comes closest to the type of place where you lived 5 YEARS AGO? MARK ONE.   1. metropolis over 1,000,000   2. suburb of a metropolis   3. large city (250,000 to 1,000,000)   4. suburb of a large city   5. medium city (50,000 to 250,000)   6. suburb of a medium city   7. small city (10,000 to 50,000)   8. town of 2,500 to 10,000   9. rural town (under 2,500)   10. rural or farm (open country)*

140. How many times have you changed residence (moved) in the past 10 years? (Mark "0" if you have not moved and skip to question 142.) _____

141. In which states have you had residence in the past 10 years?

_____

142. After your *most recent* residence change, approximately how many months passed before you: (Enter "x" if no change was necessary.)   *Changed physicians,   Changed banks/savings and loans/credit union/etc.,   Registered to vote,   Changed congregation membership,   Made nonwork acquaintances, Made one new close friendship,   Felt "at home" at new residence*
[Interval options listed were: not needed, 0-3 months, 4-8 months, 9-12 months, 12-24 months, over 24 months.]

FAMILY FINANCIAL INFORMATION

As churches do their planning it is helpful to have some information about the financial situation of the members. These questions are necessary so that the church can understand the financial base from which programs can be developed. Because some people might feel these questions are a bit personal, we again state that your answers are kept confidential. In fact, we will destroy any possible link between your name and your answers after the questionnaire is returned and before the data is analyzed.

In answering these questions you may need to contact other members of your family.

144. What is your *total family income* from all sources in 1979— before taxes? MARK ONE   *1. Under $5,000   2. $5,000-$6,999   3. $7,000-$9,999   4. $10,000-$11,999   5. $12,000-$14,999   6. $15,000-$17,999   7. $18,000-$19,999   8. $20,-000-$21,999   9. $22,000-$24,000   10. $25,000-$29,999   11. $30,000-$34,999   12. $35,000-$49,999   13. $50,000 or more*

145. During the past year what would you estimate to be your TOTAL FAMILY money contribution to your congregation? MARK ONE   *1. Less than $156   2. $156 to $259   3. $260 to $363   4. 364 to $519   5. $520 to $779   6. $780 to $1,039   7. $1,040 to $1,299   8. $1,300 to $1,559   9. $1,560 to $2,079   10. $2,080 to $2,599   11. $2,600 or more*

146. How do you decide how much to give to the church? MARK ONE THAT *BEST* DESCRIBES   *1. Use a percentage of my income   2. I choose an amount for that year based upon the prior year   3. Each week or month I decide what I can afford   4. Usually I give some of whatever I have when I attend church   5. Give as needs of the congregation arise   6. Other*

149. Pledging is the practice of committing an amount of money to give regularly to one's congregation. These pledges are then used in budgeting or financial planning. Please circle the appropriate number to indicate *your* general attitude toward pledging. CIRCLE ONE NUMBER IN EACH
    Do not see any value 1 2 3 4 5 *Pledging is necessary*
    Refuse to pledge   1 2 3 4 5 *Gladly make a pledge*

151. Do you have a will?
    Yes. If yes, are you leaving anything to the church?   *1. Yes   2. No* If no, when you have a will written do you think that

you would leave anything to the church? *3. Yes 4. Never thought about it 5. No*

156. Approximately how many dollars in a typical year do you annually, directly donate to: *Directly to national Lutheran programs, Lutheran social service or charities, Lutheran schools or colleges, Non-Lutheran educational institutions, Religious non-Lutheran causes (i.e., TV programs, Bible translators, etc.), United Fund, Medical charities, Other charities or causes*

[Dollar options listed were: $0, Less than $20, $20-$50, $51-$100, $101-$500, $501-$1000, Over $1000.]

OTHER INFORMATION

157. *If you personally* were to encounter any of the problems listed below, please indicate where you would *first* turn for help in resolving each problem if it occurred. MARK ONE FOR EACH PROBLEM *No one Family Friend Pastor Private Counsel Government Agency*
Close family death
Severe marital problems
Family alcoholism/drug abuse
Unemployment
Paralysis/retardation
Severe money problems
Unwanted pregnancy

160. Which religious magazines do you receive in your residence, and how thoroughly do you read each of them? Seldom open, Skim titles, Read 1 or 2 articles, Read whole issue
Christianity Today
Decisions
Guideposts
Christian Herald
Christian Century
church body publications were listed

The next group of questions uses the same type of format as the 1980 U.S. Census form. *Column A* contains the questions. *Column B* contains answers which apply to THE HEAD OF HOUSEHOLD. The remaining columns are for information about the spouse (if present) and any children who are economic dependents in the family (exclude grown children living on their own).

COLUMN A	COLUMN B	[Identical Columns C-K provide for other persons in household]
To make it easier to use this form, you might like to put each person's initials at the top of each column	Household Head	
166. How is this person related to household head?	(Skip for household head)	__ Husband/wife __ Son/daughter __ Brother/sister __ Father/mother __ Other
167. Sex	__ Male __ Female	__ Male __ Female
168. Age in years	_____	_____
169. Current marital status	__ Now married __ Widowed __ Divorced __ Separated __ Never married	__ Now married __ Widowed __ Divorced __ Separated __ Never married
170. Percent of total family income each provides. This line *totals* to 100%. Enter "0" if none.	_____%	_____%
171. In a typical *month*, how frequently does each person attend a worship service?	__ Once or less __ 2 or 3 times __ 4 or 5 times __ More than 5	__ Once or less __ 2 or 3 times __ 4 or 5 times __ More than 5
172. In a typical nonsummer month, how often does each person attend Sunday school or Bible class?	__ Once or less __ 2 or 3 times __ 4 or 5 times __ More than 5	__ Once or less __ 2 or 3 times __ 4 or 5 times __ More than 5

Answer also for adults

Appendix C
Profiles of Lutherans Data

The data from the Profiles of Lutherans survey exists in two types. There are data tables for each question which include age, sex, and geographic region breakdowns. There are also magnetic data tapes which contain the actual responses.

Access to the data is possible through the following sources.

Full Lutheran Data on the Core Questions

Dr. Alan C. Klaas
Aid Association for Lutherans
Appleton, WI 54919
414-734-5721

Individual Church Body Data

American Lutheran Church
Rev. Robert S. Hoyt
422 South Fifth Street
Minneapolis, MN 55415
612-330-3100

Association of Evangelical Lutheran Churches
  Mr. Elwyn Ewald
  12015 Manchester Road
  St. Louis, MO 63131
  314-821-3889

Association of Free Lutheran Congregations
  Rev. Kenneth Moland
  3110 East Medicine Lake Blvd.
  Minneapolis, MN 55441
  612-544-9501

Church of the Lutheran Brethren
  Rev. J. H. Levang
  529 Alcott Avenue, West
  Fergus Falls, MN 56537
  218-736-7404

Evangelical Lutheran Synod
  Dr. Neelak Tjernagel
  16 Lilac Drive, No. 2
  Rochester, MN 14620
  716-271-2138

Lutheran Church in America
  Rev. Dr. Albert L. Harversat
  231 Madison Avenue
  New York, NY 10016
  212-481-9600

Lutheran Church–Missouri Synod
  Mr. John O'Hara
  500 North Broadway
  St. Louis, MO 63102
  314-231-6969

Wisconsin Evangelical Lutheran Synod
  Pastor Norman W. Berg
  3512 West North Avenue
  Milwaukee, WI 53208
  414-445-4030